STOP Crying!

Get Up and Take Action

Moises Olivares

Edited by Dr. Cesar Vargas

Copyright © 2016 All Rights Reserved. Todos los Derechos Reservados. Moises Olivares. Edited by César Vargas, Ph.D.

Editing & Formatting: Dr. Cesar Vargas

Cover Design: Cesar Vargas, Ph.D.

No part of this book may be reproduced, stored in a retrieval system, or transmitted by any means, electronic, mechanical, photocopying, recording, or otherwise, without written permission from the publisher. No patent responsibility is assumed with regards to the use of the information contained herein, as this content is presented for informational and entertainment purposes only. Although every care has been taken in preparation of this book, the publisher and the author do NOT assume any responsibility for errors or omissions. In addition, no responsibility is assumed for any damages that may take place by the use of the information contained herein. Use at your own risk. The information contained herein does NOT replace the competent advice of a licensed legal, medical or mental health professional.

Visit MoisesOlivares.com to learn about our live trainings on different Success Topics!

Veritas Invictus Publishing

8502 East Chapman Avenue # 302

Orange, California 92869

ISBN 978-1-939180-04-9

www.MoisesOlivares.com

WHAT OTHERS ARE SAYING ABOUT *STOP CRYING*...

It's time to *Stop Crying! Get Up and Take Action.* Moises gives you guided action steps to accomplish your goals. The real people's stories bring home the fact that, if they can do it, YOU can accomplish anything you set your mind to. ~RUBEN MATA, World Peace Ambassador, International Speaker, and Author of *STAND* (**StandWithRuben**.com)

Moises Olivares is a very talented speaker, coach and author who, by his actions, has demonstrated how someone from such humble beginnings did not give up to reach his dreams, took action to make his goals a reality. This is an enlightening, inspiring guide for anyone interested in developing a positive attitude and achieving more in life. ~ILEANE GAXIOLA, Broker/Owner of *Century 21 Champions* and Founder of *Women Fight for Your Being*, an organization that helps women reach higher levels in life.

If you feel like life is giving up on you, the real stories of the real people in this book will afford you lots of motivation to overcome any obstacle. The motivation from this book made me believe that if I never give up on what I want, I will get it. ~JUAN RAMON SALDANA; Owner of *Newest Insurance*

This book is full of content, empowerment and, above all, implemented faith, and it gave me more determination, helped me to be more congruent and consistent, and helped me continue with my perseverance. If you're looking to improve your life, this book is for you. I personally know Moises Olivares, and he is an awesome individual with a great future. ~AMADO HERNANDEZ, Real Estate Owner/Broker

If you want to make changes in your life, but you're not sure how to do it, this book is excellent for you. It guides you through the process step by step, in a very understandable way. The many outstanding stories and quotes emphasize the messages in each chapter. I particularly liked the personal stories that showed how people from different backgrounds and experiences had the courage to change and to become successful, in spite of the hardships they may have endured. To be successful, you need to take action, and this book helps you do that by answering very thought-provoking questions at the end of each chapter. ~SANDRA P. DUNNING, DTM, PDG-District One Toastmasters, M.S. in Healthcare Management, Rehab Director at Presbyterian Intercommunity Hospital

DEDICATION

This book is dedicated to my wife Jackie for standing beside me throughout my career. My wife and my children, Alyssa and Jacklyn, have been my inspiration and motivation to continue to improve my knowledge and move my career forward. They are my rock, and I dedicate this book to them.

To my parents, Porfirio and Ofelia, for bringing me into this world, and making me the man I am today, and for teaching me the principles I now live by. To my brothers: Gabriel, Adrian, Germain, Vicente, and Jesus for helping me when I needed it the most, and to my sisters, Veronica and Diana.

Thank you to the following individuals and organizations who, without their contributions and support, this book would not have been written:

Bob and Sandy Dunning: For always inspiring me and supporting me in my speaking career and especially for believing in me since day one.

Alejandro Omana: For being my friend and showing me thorough his example what a real leader does in pursuit of a goal.

Alex Alaniz: For supporting me in my career and for inviting me to his radio show, *Real Estate Rant*.

Alfonso Silva: For encouraging me to start speaking in public and for helping me to discover the true potential that was in me and I was not capable to see on my own.

Rafael Mijangos: For believing in me, for being the person who inspired me to become a public speaker, and for allowing me to use his office to give my first speech.

Toastmasters International: For being a great organization that helped me to develop my speaking skills thorough their leadership program.

Contents

Foreword xiii

Introduction 1

   The Formula for Change

   Questions to Get You Thinking

   Why I Wrote this Book

   The Book's Format

Chapter 1: Why Do You Think the Way You Think 3

   I Was the Worst Pessimist

   What Changed My Way of Thinking?

   Having the Right Mindset

   Eagles and Chickens

   You Must Create Your Own Success

   Who Are You? - Your First Exercise

Chapter 2: The Power of Example 9

   I Didn't Care Where I Was Going, Until I Turned Around and Saw Who Was Following Me

   The Importance of the Wright brothers' Example

   How Do You Make the Impossible, Possible?

Chapter 3: Have Courage 13

    The Essential Ingredient if You Want to Change the World

    Sylvester Stallone's Story

    How to Overcome Circumstances

    The Importance of Dreaming

    What Separates Winners from Losers?

Chapter 4: Develop Character 19

    Reputation vs. Character

    How Do You Develop Character

    The Origins of Change

    If You Don't Want People to Take Advantage of You, Do This

    Is Your Character Strong or Weak?

Chapter 5: Where You Are Is Just the Starting Point 25

    The "If Only…" Syndrome

    Down and Out, and Getting Out

    Feed Your Mind Like You'd Feed a Thoroughbred Racehorse

    When I Thought Nothing Could Get Worse… Not $1.00

    The Comeback Is Sweet

    Believe in Yourself First

    Probing Questions

Chapter 6: Beliefs Are Everything 31

    Samuel's Beliefs were Greater than his Circumstances

    Samuel's Success was a Home Run

    The Origin of our Beliefs

    How Can You Change Your Beliefs?

Chapter 7: Be Prepared to Pay the Price 37

    Regular Price Vs. Luxury Price

    Successful People Understand This…

    The Price of a Nobel Prize

    The Best Moment to Give Up…

    Planning for Your Achievements

Chapter 8: Never Lose Hope 43

    When Failure Is Success in Disguise

    Success Is on the Other Side of Failure – The Story of Magnífico

    Patience and Perseverance Are Paramount

Chapter 9: Your Image Is Important 49

    People DO Judge a Book by its Cover

    We All Have Prejudices

    I Have a Challenge for You…

    Are You a Mario or Are You a Greg

    The Importance of Your Image

CHAPTER 10: TRAIN YOUR MIND FOR SUCCESS 57

    The Main Reason it's so Difficult to Change

    What Can We Do to Get Better Results?

    The Truth about Reality

    When Humor Isn't Your Thing, and You Have to Be Funny

    Jim Rohn's Story of Transformation by a Single Incident

    Success Is Something that is Learned

    Keep Your Mind Busy

    Your Mind Is like a Muscle

CHAPTER 11: HAVE FAITH 65

    On Your Journey of Success, Pack Courage, Character and Faith

    Why Most People Fail

    You May Be So Close to Your Goal

    If People Call You Crazy…

    If You're Going through a Difficult Period, Know This

CHAPTER 12: BECOME A PERSON OF GOOD HABITS 71

    What Do All Successful People Have in Common?

    Always Be On Time

    Do Not Procrastinate

    Honor Your Word

    Smile

    Always Talk Positively

CHAPTER 13: THE PRICE OF SUCCESS 79

    The Nice Thing about Success

    Two Things I'd Never Thought Would Happen to Me

    The Lowest Point in My Life!

    When People Tell You to Get a *Real* Job

CHAPTER 14: THE FIRST STEPS ARE ALWAYS THE HARDEST 87

    Why People Fail to Take Action

    A Multi-Million Dollar Mistake

    Start, So the Conditions Will Get Better

    I Didn't Want to Be a Coward in Front of My Girlfriend

    Life Is Not Easy

CHAPTER 15: MAKE SUCCESS YOUR PRIORITY 93

    What Are the Priorities in Your Life?

    Four Requirements for Success

CHAPTER 16: YOU WILL NEVER MAKE PEOPLE HAPPY 101

    A Man, His Son, and the Donkey

    Get Started Today

    Dare to Be Different… Dare to Be Yourself

CHAPTER 17: USE THE TOOLS PROPERLY 107

    You're Already Using the Tools for Success

    The Proper Way to Use the Tools

CHAPTER 18: THE ONLY WAY YOU'LL REACH SUCCESS IS IF YOU 113

    Never Listen to Gossip

    Never Say *Yes*, When You Really Want to Say *No*

    The Consequences of Not Saying *No* Can Get You in Trouble

    Never Arrive Late… My Strategy for ALWAYS Being On Time

    Never Interrupt Others

    Get Rid of Resentment

CHAPTER 19: STEPS TO REACH YOUR GOAL 123

    Make a Plan to Accomplish Your Goal

    Take Action

    Believe in Yourself

    Prepare for the Obstacles

ABOUT THE AUTHOR 127

GET TRAINED BY MOISES 129

FOREWORD

&

I ENJOYED THIS BOOK SO MUCH. As a manager and coach of one of the most successful Real Estate offices in the world, I'm constantly in search of books, ideas and tools for motivating my agents, and this book is one that can actually support my ideas.

I enjoy very much the real-life examples that you use to bring forth an idea, whether it be for creating a change in someone's life or the improvement of a situation. It seems that we are living our lives through situations, instead of a plan.

This book illustrates with examples and true events in people's lives that certainly may and will change whatever circumstances they are dealt.

I especially like the questions asked after every chapter; this is a true workbook that people can use for many different areas in their life. I am personally using this book and answering the empowering questions, and I know this will strengthen my life and make it better.

This is a book that I wholeheartedly recommend, and plan on buying several copies and giving them away as gifts, and know the recipients will use them to grow in whatever area they need in their lives.

Thank you, Moises, for the work and time you have invested to create this very thought-provoking and very helpful work.

Richard Estrada
General Manager, *CENTURY 21 Allstars*
www.C21Allstars.com

INTRODUCTION

☙

THE FORMULA FOR CHANGE IS COURAGE + CHARACTER. In this book you will find general and personal examples on how to build a strong character, how to have courage and self-confidence, and you will learn how to overcome any obstacles you might find on the road to your success.

Do you find yourself unable to say *no* to things you don't really want to do?

Have you ever quit doing something just because somebody told you that he or she didn't believe in you?

Have you started a project and abandoned it right after you found the first obstacle?

The book you're holding in your hands contains the tools that will help you develop a strong character so you can say *yes* to what you really want to do and *no* to what you don't. You'll also find tools that will help you ignore other people's opinions, become a confident person and deal with difficult times.

I wrote this book because I felt the need to share my experience and help others who are probably in the same situation I was in some time ago. When I was selling shaved iced on the streets of Los Angeles, I was a very shy and insecure person; but after building character I became a very confident person and, as a result, now I'm an author and public speaker.

In each chapter of this book you will find real stories of success; some of these stories will show you how important is to believe in yourself, the importance of always trying one more time before giving up and how to overcome difficult situations, such as being about to be evicted, ending up homeless, and the importance of being patient and courageous.

If you are ready to start your road to success, I encourage you to continue reading.

Chapter 1: Why Do You Think the Way You Think?

HAVE YOU EVER THOUGHT ABOUT WHY YOU THINK THE WAY YOU THINK, or what determines your way of thinking?

In this chapter I am going to share with you part of my story and what changed my way of thinking. If you want to show someone how to do something, it's better to do so once you've already done it.

One day while I was attending a training one of the attendees questioned the credibility of the speaker. He said, "Who is this guy? What is his level of education, or what titles does he have? Do you know if he even went to university?" My answer was, "No, but for me, none of that is important, because I don't have any of that either, and I want to learn from someone who was in the same situation I am today but found a way out and became successful. I don't just like to learn from someone who had everything in life and never faced the challenges that people like the speaker and I have faced."

Isn't it true that the easiest way to get somewhere is to ask (or learn from someone) who has already been there? In life, it's exactly the same.

For many years I lived frustrated, hating the world, hating myself and questioning my existence. I just couldn't understand why I was a failure. Every time I tried to do something to do better in life, I failed miserably. Every single time I failed, I beat myself up by telling myself things like, "You are so stupid, why did you even try? Don't you know you are good for nothing? When are you going to understand that you are a failure and that you will die as a failure?"

That was my way of thinking. So, what determined that way of thinking? I used to think that way because of my background, because of what I learned from my family, the people that surrounded me and the information to which I was exposed.

I grew up seeing my parents work hard and always short of money. Some of the phrases I heard were, "We can't afford it. That is too expensive. That's only for rich people and we are not rich." I grew up thinking that was what life was like, and I could not change it, because that was what God wanted for me.

WHAT CHANGED MY WAY OF THINKING?

In the year 2001, I joined a network marketing company. When I joined the company I had no idea what personal development was, but I was looking for something that could change my life. I committed myself and attended all the trainings they had. One day, while I was in one of those trainings the speaker asked me, "Moises, can I ask you a question?" My first thought was, "Besides being a speaker, this guy must be a mind reader; or else how does he know my name? Then I realized I had a name tag on my shirt. At the same time I thought, "Why does he have to ask ME something, when there are over 100 people in the room?" Now I thank him for asking me the question, because I am sure that, otherwise, the impact would have not been the same.

His question was, "Moises, was your great-grandfather a successful person?" "No," I said. "What about your grandfather? Was he successful, Moises?" "No," I answered again. "What about your dad? Is your dad a successful person?" "NO," was my reply once more. Right at that moment, the speaker took a step back and said to me, "Moises, I would be surprised if the answer was 'yes' because if your great-grandfather was not successful, your grandfather is not successful, and your dad is not successful, why would *you* have to be successful? But, I have good news for you," he said. "As the independent individual that you are, you can take charge of yourself, take action and change your future. Your success will be determined by the books you read, the information you are exposed to, and the people you hang around with."

His words gave me what I needed: Hope. Before hearing his words, I was hopeless; I just didn't know what I wanted to do or what I could do. That day, my life literally changed. I had just discovered that I could do a lot more than I thought I was capable of. I knew it wasn't going to be easy, but I also knew it was possible.

As with everything else, in the beginning it was not easy. When I began to try to change things, they would still come out wrong. But now I was aware of what was happening. I knew it was just part of the game. Lasting and powerful changes do not happen overnight. Every time things did not come out right, I would laugh and tell myself, "It's just part of the process."

When you have the wrong mindset, it is as if you were blind, because you don't see the positive things and the opportunities that surround you, simply because your mind is tuned into the "Impossible frequency."

Let me tell you a story that illustrates how serious it could be when you don't know your true potential or who you are.

There's an old, well-known story of a chicken farmer who found an eagle's egg. He put it with his chickens and soon the egg hatched.

The young eagle grew up with all the other chickens, and whatever they did, the eagle did too. He thought he was a chicken, just like them.

Since the chickens could only fly for a short distance, the eagle also learned to fly a short distance. He thought that was what he was supposed to do, so that was all he thought he could do. As a result, that was all he was able to do.

One day, the eagle looked up and saw a bird flying high above him. He was very impressed. "Who is that?" he asked the hens around him.

"That's the eagle, the king of the birds," the hens told him. "He belongs to the sky. We belong to the earth, we are just chickens."

So the eagle lived and died as a chicken, for that's what he thought he was.

How many times have you given up on something just because someone told you that you were not capable of doing it, or because you listened to other people's opinions?

If you want to change your future you have to know who you are, and what you are capable of. Let the chickens be chickens. Get away from them; you are an Eagle!

When you surround yourself with positive-minded people, people who know how to make things happen, inevitably you will learn from them.

You only become good at what you train for. Tiger Woods cannot throw away his clubs today, and join the Dodgers tomorrow, and expect to hit a home run at his first turn at bat. Could he become a good baseball player? Of course he can, but he has to train in that area.

What determines your way of thinking?

1. The environment that surrounds you
2. The information you are exposed to
3. What you see and what you hear

If you do not like the environment that surrounds you, the information you are exposed to, and what you see and hear, look for new friends; surround yourself with positive people, read books, watch inspirational movies, and listen to motivational and self-improvement audios.

Now that you know what determines your way of thinking, answer the following questions:

Why do you think you think the way you think?

_____
_____
_____

How would you like to think?

_____
_____
_____

How is the environment you are in right now?

_____
_____
_____

What environment would you like to be in?

_____

_____

_____

What programs or materials are you currently watching? Are you reading books? Is the information you are listening to positive or negative?

_____

_____

_____

What type of programs are you going to start watching, what type of books are you going to start reading, and what type of information are you going to start listening to from now on?

_____

_____

_____

Chapter 2:
The Power of Example

&

Have you ever asked yourself how powerful *example* is? It's scientifically proven that we learn by imitation. We tend to act accordingly to the people around us. Think about it for a moment, I'm sure that, as a kid, you had a hero in your life. That hero was probably your father, your mother, one of your older siblings, or maybe one of your uncles. Do you remember who it was? Isn't it true that you wanted to talk like that person, walk like that person, and be just like that person? The people that surround you have a lot of influence on you, and you tend to do what those people around you do, even if what they are doing doesn't make sense. Let me give you an example of how your hero can help you to be successful or how that hero can hold you back.

Joe was a cook at a restaurant and he was a hero to his 3-year-old son. Joe says that one day he got home after work and sat on his couch. He was really tired, feeling hopeless and trapped at a job he hated, but what else could he do? He didn't know any better. Joe had placed his apron and his chef hat on the corner of the couch. Remember, Joe was his son's hero, and his son wanted to be just like his hero—his dad. So the little boy ran, grabbed his dad's apron and chef hat, and put them on. Then he started saying, "Yeah! When I grow up, I am going to be just like my dad. I am going to cook a lot of hamburgers, burritos and fries." Joe says that he felt so bad to see his son doing and saying those things, and he thought to himself, "Is this what I want for my son? What kind of an example am I being for him? What am I showing him? I have to do something about it." Joe knew he had to make changes in his life, so he made a decision. If he wanted a better future for himself and his son, he needed to change. Joe went to a training that helped him change his mindset, and this helped him so much that he ended up co-writing a book, and he became a public speaker.

Now, instead of the apron and the chef hat, when Joe comes home he puts his suit and tie on the corner of the same couch.

Joe still is his son's hero. The difference is that now when Joe comes home, his son runs to put on his dad's suit and tie and says, "Yeah! When I grow up, I'm going to be just like my dad. I'm going to write lots of books and give a lot of speeches around the world."

As you can see, Joe's son didn't change at all, he still wants to be like his dad; the difference is that before, when Joe was a cook, his son wanted to be a cook; now that Joe is an author and public speaker, his son wants to be an author and public speaker, just like his dad.

There's a phrase by an unknown author that says, "Words can convince you, but the example will drag you." And this is true. Not long ago, I was watching the news and heard the anchor say that the police had arrested two people that were caught shoplifting. What called my attention was the fact that these two people were father and son. That's right; they were a father and son thief team. This made me think. *Hmm! How is it that, while Joe's son is thinking of becoming an author and public speaker, this other son decided to become a criminal?* That's right, you guessed—the example; the examples each of these kids were exposed to have influenced their life choices. For each of these kids, their parents are their heroes, and all they are trying to do is to be like their dads.

If you want your life to change, you have to be like a kid; you have to look for new heroes. Think about a person you admire, a person who has achieved or created something that amazes you. Some of my heroes are the Wright brothers. The reason is because the Wright brothers broke a paradigm; they went against logic, they went against the world's mindset at that time, and made an object fly, when everyone else believed that was just not possible. At the time the Wright brothers achieved their goal, it was an established and accepted *fact* that nothing heavier than the air could fly, except for the birds. That paradigm was something everyone had accepted as a fact for thousands of years. That's why I have the Wright brothers as some of my heroes; they made something possible that the rest of the world thought was impossible.

It is said your success will be determined by the books you read and the people you surround yourself with.

Look around and see if the people you are surrounding yourself with are the way you would like to be in the future. Read as many books as possible, feed your spirit and your soul with positive information every day. Books can change your life, literally. Books change not only your mindset, but they also change the way you walk, the way you talk and even the way you dress. One of the things I mention during my speeches is the fact that I was not the way I am today my whole life; if there was someone that was negative in this world that was me. I knew all the rules that worked to make things not work. My self-esteem was on the floor and I had no communication skills at all. I never thought I was going to be speaking in public; writing a book one day was something that was out of the question. It didn't fit in my narrow mind.

I don't know what your state of mind is right at this moment, but I can tell you that no matter where you are or how you feel right now, you have the power to turn things around, even when it seems impossible.

The impossible becomes possible when you start believing in yourself and take action.

Chapter 3: Have Courage

ONE OF THE THINGS THAT DISTINGUISH SUCCESSFUL PEOPLE FROM THE REST is that successful people are very courageous.

Change requires a lot of courage. When you are trying to change, your friends, family members and coworkers will come to tell you why you should not change.

"The people who are crazy enough to think they can change the world are the ones who do." Steve Jobs

At the beginning of your change people will judge you and call you crazy for thinking differently. This is where you'll need to have enough courage to not listen to them, and do what you think is right for you. If things don't turn out the way they are supposed to, don't worry; it's just part of the process and you are not the first one who has ever failed in the pursuit of success. Read the stories of all the well-known people, like Abraham Lincoln, Walt Disney, Colonel Sanders, and many more. You'll be amazed by the number of times they failed, before becoming successful with their ideas.

All the aforementioned people achieved their goals because they had the courage to continue. Do you think they had naysayers? Of course they did, but they knew what they wanted and decided to go for it *in spite of* the naysayers.

My first job in the U.S. was as a street vendor selling shaved ice. I clearly remember a specific instance, on the day I went to apply for another job and was rejected. When I went back home, some of my "friends" were there peeling corn (as prep work, because we would also sell corn) and others getting ready to go to work, one of them said sarcastically, "Here comes the dreamer who thinks he can get a different job; they didn't give it to you huh?" Honestly, I felt very bad because the truth was that I had been rejected.

He continued his belittling mockery, "Stop dreaming! Who is going to want to hire you if you don't know anything? You are a nobody, and you don't have experience at anything."

Again, I felt very bad; I felt like a failure. Surprisingly, the very next day I received a phone call from the same place where I had been rejected. The person who had referred me there talked to the general manager and he (the general manager) had decided to give me a chance.

I must confess that, at the time, I had no courage, and my "friend's" words did affect me.

When you develop courage you don't worry anymore about what other people think or say about you. You just keep on going.

A GOOD EXAMPLE OF THAT IS SYLVESTER STALLONE.

Before Sylvester Stallone was a world-famous actor, he struggled to even manage to get by. At one point, he was so broke that he stole his wife's jewelry and sold it. Not only that, he even ended up homeless. Unable to pay rent or afford food, he slept at a New York bus station for 3 days. But he reached the lowest point of this situation when he was forced to sell his dog at a liquor store to any stranger, because he didn't have money to feed the dog anymore. He sold it for $25. He says he walked away crying, frustrated and defeated by his life circumstances.

Two weeks later, he saw a boxing match between Mohammed Ali and Chuck Wepner. That match gave him the inspiration to write the script for his famous movie, Rocky. He was so enthused that he wrote the script writing for 20 hours straight! He went to sell it and received an offer of $125,000 for the script. That was great, but he had just one request: He wanted to star in the movie.

He wanted to play the main character, Rocky Balboa himself. But the studio said no. They wanted a real star.

They turned him down saying he "looked funny and talked funny." Stallone left with his script. A few weeks later, the studio offered him $250,000 for the script, if he gave up on his idea of playing the protagonist. He refused. They offered him $350,000. He still refused. They wanted his movie, but not him. He said no. He had to be the star of that movie.

After a while, the studio decided that they were not going to risk a lot of money on an unknown, and agreed to pay him $35,000 for the script and let him star in it. The rest, as they say, is history! The movie won Best Picture, Best Directing and Best Film Editing at the prestigious Oscar Awards. He was even nominated for Best Actor! The Rocky movie was even inducted into the American National Film Registry as one of the greatest movies ever!

And, do you know what was the first thing he bought with the $35,000? The dog he sold. Yes, Stallone loved his dog so much that he stood at the liquor store for 3 days, hoping to find the man he sold his dog to. And on the 3rd day, he saw the man coming with the dog. Stallone explained why he sold the dog and begged for the dog back. The man refused. Stallone offered him $100. The man refused. He offered him $500. And the guy refused. Yes, he refused even $1000. As the legend goes, Stallone paid the man $15,000 (and gave him a small part in his movie) for the same dog he sold for $25, and he finally got his dog back!

And today, the same Stallone who slept in the streets and sold his dog just because he couldn't even feed it anymore is one of the greatest Movie Stars who ever walked the Earth! Here is some of his wisdom:

Being broke is bad… really bad. Have you ever had a dream, a wonderful dream, but you are too broke to implement it, too tiny to do it, too small to accomplish it?

Life is tough. Opportunities will pass you by, just because you are a nobody. People will want your products but not you. It's a tough world, if you are not already famous or rich or "connected," you will find it rough.

Doors will be shut on you; people will steal your glory and crush your hopes, you will push and push, and yet nothing will happen.

And then your hopes will be crushed. You'll be broke, damn broke; you'll do odd jobs for survival; you'll be unable to feed yourself; and yes, you might end up sleeping on the streets, it happens. Yes, it does.

But never let them crush that dream. Whatever happens to you, keep dreaming. Even when they crush your hopes, keep dreaming. Even when they turn you down, keep dreaming. Even when they shut you down, keep dreaming.

No one knows what you are capable of, except yourself! People will judge you by how you look and by what you have, but fight on! Fight for your place in history; fight for your glory. In the words of Winston Churchill, "Never, ever, ever give up!"

Even if it means selling all of your clothes and sleeping with the dogs, it's okay! But as long as you are still alive, your story is not over.

Keep up the fight! Keep your dreams and hopes alive! Go get it!!!

This is what I call courage! As you can see, Stallone had many other options, including receiving a good amount of money for his film script. But he was determined and was not going to settle for less; all the odds were against him including his "impediments," but he had courage; he did not listen to what other people said to him; he kept on going and, as a result of that, he achieved his goal. What would have happened if he was not courageous enough? I guarantee you that nobody would know who he is.

Courage is what separates winners from losers; losers think it is impossible and quit. Winners know it will not be easy but it is possible and keep going until they get what they want.

As you can see, the price of success is not low; that's why most people quit. Most of them quit at the beginning, as soon as they see that it's not as easy as they thought.

Answer the following questions to determine how fervently you want to achieve your goal.

What is it that you want to achieve in life?

_____

_____

_____

What are you going to do when you face the first obstacle?

_____

_____

_____

What are you going to do if things still don't work out again, and again and again?

_____
_____
_____

What are going to do when you get rejected?

_____
_____
_____

When are you going to stop trying?

_____
_____
_____

On a scale of one to ten, with ten being the highest, at what level do you consider your courage is? Circle one.

1   2   3   4   5   6   7   8   9   10

Chapter 4: Develop Character

෩

John Wooden said, "Your reputation is who people think you are; your character is who you really are."

How many times have you quit doing something just because of your lack of character? You were probably too worried about what the people around you might think or say about you, and you decided to not do anything instead.

I think we all have gone thorough that at least once in our lives, but why does that happen?

It happens because we are so insecure, and our lack of character stops us from making our decisions and we end up asking others for advice. The problem is that, many times, those "others" we ask for advice are in the same situation we are in—or even worse.

The Wright brothers are a good example of the difference between reputation and character. The Wrights had a reputation for being crazy because they wanted to make an object fly. At the time, that was a crazy idea because according to the experts nothing heavier than air could fly, except for the birds.

The Wright brothers had character; they didn't give up and they proved the world wrong. Their first flight was considered a failure because the plane stayed in the air for just 12 seconds and covered only 120 feet. Just imagine what would have happened if the Wright brothers didn't have their character developed. Planes simply would not exist.

How do you develop character?

You must acquire knowledge. That's right; when you're a knowledgeable person people respect you.

At the beginning of my career as a car salesman, I remember that my clients were very rude to me. They would tell me how much they wanted to pay for the car, the interest rate they thought they deserved, how much of a down payment they wanted to pay, and how much they wanted to pay per month. Because I didn't know the business, I could not overcome all of the objections they gave me. I didn't have the character to make them understand it was not about what they wanted but about what was possible to do.

Books and audios about sales was the key. I read some books about sales, listened to some audios about the different types of closings there are. All of that helped me understand that if I wanted to sell more I needed to develop character, or else my sales were going to stay on the floor.

Once I developed my character I was able to defend myself from my clients.

At the beginning, when a client would ask, "What is the price of this car, how much of a down payment do I need, or what would my monthly payment be?" right after I answered all those questions the clients would turn to me and say things like, "The price is too high, why would you want so much down payment, and why is my monthly payment so high?" my only answer was, "That's what the manager wants."

My clients did not change; I did. After acquiring knowledge and feeling more comfortable, I remember getting the exact same objections, but now I was prepared.

I had a client who wanted to buy a car, but the problem was that his credit was not so good; therefore, he didn't qualify for the loan. He was also demanding a low interest rate and a low monthly payment. This time, instead of being afraid, I told him, "I understand you want to buy a nice car, but the thing is that there is no way we can get the loan approved with any of the banks available. The only thing you can do in your situation is to buy a cheaper car to improve your credit; that way, in a year or two from now you will be qualified to finance the car you want." "I'd rather wait," he said.

"That's not a problem," I told him. "The thing is, if you wait one or two more years and you haven't done anything to improve your credit, my answer will be the same. If you buy the car I am recommending that you buy today, you make your payments on time for a year or two and then come back to me, then I'll be able to get you approved for the car that you want."

"But you're asking a lot of money for the down payment, and the interest you are giving me is very high," he said.

Remember I had character now so I told him, "You're probably right, but let me explain to you what happens. Remember that you only qualify for a certain amount to be financed. This means that whatever amount exceeds what the bank is qualifying you for, you have to pay in cash. Now, you're telling me the interest rate is high; let me explain something to you. The interest rate is based on your FICO score. The FICO score is what tells the banks how good you are at paying loans. And you know that your credit is not great, right?"

"Right," he said.

"If it were up to me," I told him, "I'd give you the lowest interest rate there is, but unfortunately I can't. But things are very easy: This is what you qualify for. I just need you to tell me whether you agree to it or not."

He (the client) thought about it for a moment and asked, "So, you're telling me that if I buy the car you are recommending, and I come back in two years I can get the car I want, right?"

"Right, as long as you make your payments on time," I said. "OK. I'm going to buy the car you are recommending." And… deal closed!

As you can see, in the beginning I didn't have the character to tell my clients things the way they were; but after acquiring knowledge, I was able to negotiate with the clients, because I now had the right arguments to help them understand I was there to sell, but they couldn't buy what they wanted under their own terms.

When your character is weak, people take advantage of you. Don't let that happen. Work hard on yourself and develop a strong character.

Whether you are in sales or not, you need to build a strong character, so others won't use you. A strong character will help you to say 'no' to those who try to make you do things that you really don't want to do.

What would you like to have done, but you didn't do it because you cared more about your reputation?

_____

_____

If your character is not at its best, what do you think caused that situation?

_____

_____

What are you going to do to develop character? Be specific.

_____

_____

_____

How are you going to react the next time you have the opportunity to do something that will require showing character?

_____

_____

_____

How do you visualize yourself once you have developed character?

_____

_____

_____

How do you think developing character will impact not only your life, but your family and your future generations?

_____

_____

_____

Chapter 5: Where You Are Is Just the Starting Point

THE MAIN REASON PEOPLE DON'T ACHIEVE THEIR GOALS is mainly because they think it is impossible to make them happen, due to the situation they are in. This is the way the majority of the people who are in a bad situation think, "If only I had enough money to start my own business, my life would be so different. If my family would support me, it would be easier for me to achieve my goal." The truth is that your future is not determined by your current situation; your current situation is just the starting point.

There are many stories of people, who reached success having nothing in their pockets. The only thing they had was faith, and nothing else. That is the case of Carlos Cobian.

Carlos Cobian is a Real Estate Agent at a very important Century 21 Real Estate office in Pico Rivera, California. Carlos used to work for a retail store, stocking merchandise. He was sick and tired of that job because he felt he was going nowhere, and his financial situation was really bad. He knew he needed to do something about it, but he didn't know what.

Carlos decided to join the real estate business, but things were not easy for him. The first sale he made was in the city of Big Bear, California. He sold a cabin for $42,000; his commission… $500.

That's right, his first commission was only $500. After that, he closed a couple more transactions, but nothing significant.

Months went by and Carlos could not close anything else. One day while he was working he received a call. The person at the other end of the line was one of his two kids. His son told him, "Dad, we are home but we can't open the door."

Carlos knew he was behind with his rent, so he figured out that the landlord had changed the locks. Now Carlos and his two kids were homeless. Carlos went to pick up his kids and they camped out in the parking lot of the office he was working for.

Time went on, and although he was working hard he couldn't close anything for almost six months. Carlos and his two kids were homeless for more than five months. He says that when he would get some money he and his two sons would stay in a motel but that was once in a while. The rest of the time he and his two kids were living in a minivan out in the office's parking lot.

What helped Carlos to keep on going during the time he was homeless was the fact that he was always positive. He would read a lot and talk to his kids about how their lives were going to be once they got out of the situation they were in. Carlos would talk to his kids about inspirational movies, movies like *The Pursuit of Happiness* and *Million Dollar Baby*.

After months of hard work, a lot of tears, ups and downs Carlos finally closed a couple of transactions that put over $60,000 in his pocket, and he hasn't stopped closing deals ever since.

As you can see, all throughout this time Carlos had a clear vision of what he wanted. Was it easy? Of course not! He says that he thought about going back to his old job because the pressure was huge, and at times it looked like it was never going to end. But he didn't give up. Instead, he kept on going; he never lost his enthusiasm and hope. He paid the price and received his reward.

When I heard Carlos's story, I identified myself with him, especially the part where he was evicted. Luckily, I've never been evicted, but I was very close to it. I think the only reason the landlord didn't evict us was because of our little girls, who at the time were six and three.

When the real estate market crashed right in the middle of the economic crisis, I lost my home and had to resort to renting a house. I didn't have a steady job and was three months behind on my rent. That was very difficult for my wife and me, since we were very responsible and had never been late with our rent. It got to the point where I spoke with the landlord and told him, "You know what? It's not that I don't want to pay you, it's just that I don't have any money. I'm going to pay you, you can be sure of that, but I don't know when. It could be next week or probably until next month. I don't know." Of course, that didn't really help because I was not giving my landlord a solution. I was practically telling him to trust me, something that was already hard for him to do, since I had told him several times before that I was going to pay him what I owed him, and I didn't. The reason I'd tell him I was going to pay him was because there were people who owed me money, and they'd tell me they were going to pay me. Therefore, every time that happened I would tell my landlord that I was not going to pay him everything, but I was going to, at least, give him something, and when the people didn't pay me, I ended up not paying him.

That was very embarrassing and humiliating for my wife and me, but at the same time there wasn't a lot we could do; we just couldn't make ends meet.

I thought nothing worse could happen to me… I was wrong.

One day, I went to pick up my six-year-old daughter from school. I was walking back home with her and my then three-year-old. There was a guy standing at the corner of our street selling chips and Alyssa, my six-year-old daughter asked me if I could buy her chips. I did want to buy them for her, but there was a big problem: I did not have a single dollar in my pocket, so I had to tell her "No." Alyssa started crying and she went into the house, still crying. She sat on the bed and through her tears she told me, "I don't like what is happening; I don't like the life we are living. I just want chips but we can never buy anything." That broke my heart and I felt hopeless and as a failure. I was not being man enough to support my family. But, what happened next cut even more deeply into my heart. Jacklyn, my three-year-old, told her big sister, "Alyssa, please understand; my dad doesn't have money to buy you chips." You can just imagine that scene—a three-year-old asking her big sister to please understand.

That was probably the lowest point for me; never mind not being able to pay the rent; to see my daughter suffering for not having enough money was much more heartbreaking.

I didn't give up; I kept on fighting and, a few weeks later, I closed a transaction where I made $20,000. The first thing I did was to go pay my rent. By this time, I was almost four months behind, which totaled $3,600. I went to see the landlord to pay him. As I was handing him the money, I could see the look of disbelief in his eyes. I told him, "I know you probably thought I wasn't going to pay you, but let me tell you that you were right to think that about me, because I wasn't paying my rent on time. I told you I was going to pay you, and here is your money. Thank you for being patient with me."

WHERE YOU ARE IS JUST THE STARTING POINT. Think big, persist, never give up and believe in yourself.

What is your current situation?

_____

_____

Are you happy with who you are and where you are?

_____

If yes, why?

_____

_____

If not, why not?_____

_____

If you are not happy where you are, what are you going to do, starting today, to change your future?

_____

_____

_____

Do you already know the obstacles you are going to have to face? What are they?_____

_____

_____

How would your life be if you achieved your goal?_____

_____

_____

What is the price you will have to pay to achieve your goal, and are you willing to pay it?

_____

_____

_____

CHAPTER 6: BELIEFS ARE EVERYTHING

"Whether you think you can, or you think you can't you're right."
— Henry Ford

THERE IS NOTHING MORE POWERFUL THAN BELIEFS. Your beliefs determine where you are in your life today.

No matter what part of the world you are in right now, if your beliefs are stronger than your limitations, you can be whoever you want or wherever you want.

When Samuel was a little boy in the Dominican Republican he used to work as a shoeshine boy. He had no shoes or clothes to wear, but he had big dreams. His belief was that, one day, he would be a professional baseball player in the major leagues in the U.S.A. His friends, family members, and coworkers would tell him he was crazy, and to stop dreaming.

Everyone who told Samuel that what he wanted was impossible. They told him that because, logically, it was impossible. But Samuel's beliefs were very strong, and he was convinced he could become a professional baseball player in the U.S.

Samuel had no doubts he could achieve his goal, so he would practice baseball every day.

Samuel was a very poor little kid. He didn't own a nice bat or a nice glove. Samuel used a piece of sugar cane as a bat; for a glove, he used a milk gallon jug that he had cut and adapted as if it were a real glove. He was always enthusiastic and nobody could make him give up his dream.

Time went on and, although Samuel heard thousands of times to stop dreaming and that his dream was never going to become true, he kept practicing with passion every day.

Samuel's dream came true when he was signed by a team in the USA. By the mid 90's Samuel had become a consistent 30-40 home run player. In 1997, he signed a four-year, $42.5 million dollar contract with the Cubs. But the really special show began in 1998. That year, Mark McGwire and Samuel (who, by now, you should have figured out is Sammy Sosa) went head-to-head to see who could hit more homeruns. McGwire had the early lead but by late August, they were going back and forth. Mark McGwire hit 70 homeruns that year, but Sammy Sosa wasn't that far behind, with 66, and both beat Roger Maris's long-standing single season record of 63 home runs in a year. That season proved to be one where Major League Baseball finally had something good going for itself, with fans clambering to get more of McGwire and Sosa. He and Mark shared Sports Illustrated magazine's 1998 "Sportsmen of the Year" award. After that frenetic year, Sammy still had a lot more still left in the tank. Over the next four seasons, he did not miss a beat.

Sammy Sosa made history. He is in the Hall of Fame as one of the best players in the history of the major leagues in the USA.

As you can see, there are no excuses; if someone who was born very poor, with no apparent opportunities or no apparent reasons to make it in life, could become successful, it means anybody in this world can achieve any goal by just believing it is possible. A belief is the most powerful force that makes things that seem impossible, possible.

At the beginning of this chapter I mentioned that your beliefs determine where you are in your life today.

Let me explain why that is.

You can only achieve, see, and have, what you think and believe is possible. Everything is possible in this world. So, what's the problem?

The problem is that we do not develop our own beliefs. When we are children, our parents teach us how to eat and how to walk, and they put into our minds what they have in theirs. If what they have is not positive, we receive that exact same information. And, based on that information, we create our own beliefs.

When I was a child, my father used to speak ill of one of our neighbors. I heard my father say so many negative things about the neighbor that I ended up believing that the person my dad was talking about was a bad person. Was my dad right? No, he wasn't. But my dad created a belief in me, without him knowing.

And the same way my dad created that belief in me, he created most of my beliefs. I grew up thinking and believing I had very bad luck, and that I was destined to live in misery my whole life.

As children, we don't have control of the people that surround us or the information we are exposed to. But as adults, as the independent individuals we are, we are 100 percent responsible for our actions and results.

If you want to change your beliefs and your results, it's necessary for you to stop doing and believing what you have been doing and believing until today.

HOW CAN YOU CHANGE YOUR BELIEFS?

Our beliefs are developed through repetition; the more we listen to the same thing, the easier it becomes for our mind to remember. A good example of this, are the different religions.

If a kid is raised in a Christian household, chances are that kid will be a Christian when he grows up. Now, what are the chances of a kid that is raised in a Catholic household to become a Catholic when he grows up? Very high chances, right? Same as the kid who was raised as a Christian. These two kids will grow up with different beliefs, and each of them will defend their religion and point of view, which is totally acceptable.

In life, it's the same thing; we believe what we were taught to believe. If those beliefs are not taking us to where we want to be, it is time to start changing those beliefs for new ones. I say "start changing" because things do not change overnight; change has a process.

The first step to start changing is to change the environment. You have to find new friends, friends who encourage you. You need to surround yourself with positive people, people who already achieved something, or are in the process to achieve it.

Think big; aim high. Once you start thinking big, you start attracting to your life other people who think alike.

Being surrounded by positive people will not only change your way of thinking, it will eventually change the way you talk, the way you act and the way you dress. Your beliefs are the result of repetition; so, now that you are exposed to all these successful people, sooner or later you will end up becoming one of them in every aspect, because *you are the result of your environment and your beliefs.*

What is your current situation?

_____

_____

What would you like to do, or who would you like to become?

_____

_____

_____

What has stopped you from taking action towards what you want?

_____

_____

What are you going to do to start changing your beliefs?

_____

_____

_____

What type of environment will be ideal for you, and where can you find that kind of environment?

_____

_____

How do you visualize yourself in one year, three years or five years from now?

_____

_____

_____

Chapter 7: Be Prepared to Pay the Price

☙

When you want something, all you have to do to obtain it is to PAY THE PRICE. You want a new TV? All you have to do is go to the electronics store, pay the price for it, and take it home. Do you want a new car? Just go to a car dealer, pay the price for the car you want, and take it home. Now, the make and model, the year, and the extras the car has will determine the price you're going to have to pay. If you want a regular car the price you pay will be lower than if you want a luxury car.

Average things are made for the majority of the people, and they are usually cheap. For example, an average car would be a Hyundai, Honda, or Toyota, just to name a few. Usually these types of cars are made for the working class, and the prices are low compared to other brands.

Now, if you want something that very few people have, you'd look into something like a Mercedes Benz, BMW or a Ferrari. The price to pay for any of those cars will be way, way higher than the price you have to pay for any other regular brand.

What do I mean by that?

What I mean by that is this. The size of your dream will determine the price you are going to have to pay for you to obtain it. If your dream is small, the price to pay will be small, as well. But if your dream is big you'd better get ready to pay a high price, a price that most people are not willing to pay. What makes successful people different from the rest? Successful people are willing to take extra risks, risks that the rest are not willing to take. A successful person understands that, in the process, he or she might lose money, but at the same time is not afraid of it, because he or she knows that there is a price to pay. *Being successful does not mean you will obtain what you want in an easy way.*

A successful person usually faces challenges and circumstances that make him or her doubt himself/herself. This is where successful people prove their mettle because, when facing those same circumstances, most people would just quit, but not you. You are not most people. You are one-of-a-kind; you are bigger than any difficulty or circumstance, and you are bigger than any obstacle. If, at any moment, you think about quitting, remember that you knew from the beginning this was not going to be easy. Also, remember that if you quit you will be remembered as a failure (that is, if you're remembered at all). Quitters don't make history; nobody knows who they were.

How big is your dream? Are you ready to pay the price?

Gabriel García Márquez was one of the most preeminent writers in the magical realism genre. Márquez won the Nobel Prize of Literature in 1982. Behind the enormous success Gabriel achieved throughout his life, there was a price he had to pay.

On June 26, 1961, Gabriel's family arrived at a railway station in Mexico City with their last $20 in their pocket, and "nothing in their future." García Márquez started writing, and in just 18 months, he'd completed the novel that would change his life. In *One Hundred Years of Solitude*, he used all of the storytelling techniques he'd picked up as a reporter. As he would later tell *The New York Times*, the "tricks you need to transform something which appears fantastic, unbelievable into something plausible, credible, those I learned from journalism. The key is to tell it straight. It is done by reporters and by country folk."

Although the writing came quickly, it was not easy. To support his family, García Márquez had to sell his car, his hair dryer, and anything else that would bring in some cash.

When the time came send off the manuscript to his publishers in Buenos Aires, Argentina, he could only afford to mail half of it.

Half was enough. With *One Hundred Years of Solitude*, García Márquez exploded onto the literary scene. While still living in Mexico, he quickly emerged as Latin America's most beloved writer and was affectionately nicknamed "Gabo." In Colombia, he became a symbol of national pride. The book would go on to sell more than 35 million copies and be translated into at least 35 languages.

For reasons unknown, successful people always have to go through difficult times before they reach success.

Just imagine what would of have happened if Gabriel García Márquez gave up on his dream because of the circumstances he and his family were going through? The world would have never known about him or who he was.

The best moment to give up is *never*.

For some reason, things turn more difficult when you are about to achieve what you have been looking for. Remember this every time you feel like giving up. It is there precisely where the majority of the people quit, most people quit right before they achieve their goal.

Always go one step further, because you never know how close you really are from your objective. And, if it doesn't happen, try again, and again, and again. Try as many times as necessary; try until you get what you want.

What would like to become?

_____

_____

Gabriel García Márquez gave up his stability in exchange for his dream; what are you willing to give up?

_____

_____

Have you ever tried to do something and you gave up when the first obstacle arrived? If yes, what was it?

_____

_____

_____

Let's say you try something many times, but things don't work out the way you expected or, even worse, it appears that what you are trying to do will never happen. What are you going to do, give up or try one more time?

_____

_____

_____

We all have ideas, but only a few take action and make things happen. When are you going to take action and make your dream come true? Put a date on your dreams.

_____

_____

_____

How would you like to be remembered, as a failure or as a person who reached success because you didn't give up, and you overcame all the obstacles?

_____

_____

_____

Remember that things always turn more difficult right when you are about to achieve your goal.

Chapter 8:
Never Lose Hope

☙

TO THIS DAY, I HAVEN'T HEARD ABOUT A SUCCESSFUL PERSON who had it easy. Sometimes you feel like just throwing everything away and going back to where you were before. For a person who is really hungry for success, quitting is not an option, although he or she could very much feel like giving up. Sometimes, things go from bad to worse in life; I have lived it, and probably you have, too. It's interesting to know that, sometimes, what we consider the worst thing that could happen to us ends up being the best things that could ever have happened to us.

There was once a castaway who was living on an island. After many attempts to go back to civilization and failing, he gave up and decided to spend the rest of his life in that island. He built a small house, made of palm trees and, for him, that was his most valuable possession. As time went on he became used to his new lifestyle, although he always wished he could go back to his family and friends. He'd go fishing every morning, and after that he would go looking for fruit to eat. This was his everyday routine. One day, while he was picking fruits, he saw smoke coming out from between the trees. He stopped doing what he was doing and ran to his little house. When he got there, he couldn't believe his eyes. His home was engulfed in flames! He felt hopeless for not being able to do anything to put out the fire. He could only watch as his most precious possession went up in smoke. He asked God, "God, why did this happen to me?" devastated, and thinking nothing worse could happen to him, he cried for hours until he fell asleep.

Hours later, he was awakened by somebody. Surprised, he asked, "How did you find me?" The man replied, "We saw the smoke signals you sent us, and we came to your rescue."

No matter how bad things look, never lose hope.

It's amazing that most successful people say that they had already lost hope and were about to give up when success finally came to their lives.

One day I was talking to someone at a gym owned by the well-known boxer, Israel Vasquez, AKA "Magnífico." The owner was around, and joined our conversation. I was talking about the importance of not giving up and about Edison's well-known phrase, "Many of life's failures are people who did not realize how close they were to success when they gave up." When Israel heard that, he said, "You know what, I can relate to that phrase. When I came to this country, I did so because I wanted to become a professional boxer, but things were not easy. I got a part-time job, and I used to live in a small room. With the money I earned, I was barely surviving. I got desperate because it wasn't what I expected, nor was it what the people who brought me here promised. When I was approached in Mexico City, I was told I was coming here to fight professionally, and that I was going to get paid. Well, I did get paid, but I would have a fight once every two or three months, and my pay was only $250 per fight, so it got to the point where I said, "You know what? I think I'm just going back to Mexico City. I'll forgo my dream and get on with my life." He said he was about to quit, right before he fought his first real fight.

That fight was the one Israel had been waiting for, and it was the first time he received a good purse as a professional boxer. How much money did he make? He made Eight Hundred Thousand Dollars!

Imagine that! He was about to lose eight hundred thousand dollars.

Be patient; you can't be anxious just because you haven't gotten the results that you wanted just yet.

Just like the castaway was rescued when he thought nothing worse could happen to him, and the way Israel's hard work and patience was rewarded, you can achieve what you want, simply by not giving up or losing hope.

I think we all have gone through difficult times. I personally stopped doing presentations for a whole year because I didn't feel that I had the right to tell people what to do to get better results when I wasn't getting the results that I wanted. One day, I was watching some videos in YouTube ™ when I came across a video of a well-known speaker. In that video, he talked about how when he was at the beginning of his career as a motivational speaker he had a presentation in the city of Palm Springs. In the video he explained how hard it was for him and his beat up Volkswagen Beetle to make it there from the Los Angeles area. He said that when he got to the city of Palm Springs he parked his car about ten blocks away from the hotel where the event was taking place. He said, "When I got into that room and saw all the professionals there waiting for me, I knew that there was not a single person in the whole room that wasn't more successful than I was. When I got on the stage and started delivering my message I felt very good. My presentation was a success. Right there I knew that I was going in the right direction because I already was who I wanted to be. I didn't have the material things that come with success yet, but they were on their way."

What he said after that was what helped me to retake my career as a public speaker. He said, "To be a successful person you first have to *be*, then *do*, so you can *have*."

You never know how long it's going to take. You just have to know that things will happen, one way or another. Don't worry about *how* things are going to happen, just concentrate on doing *your part* and the Universe will reward your effort.

There are two kinds of people in this world, the ones who quit when they face their first obstacle, and the ones who persist and overcome every single obstacle that stands in their way. Which group do you belong to?

Reaching success in not easy, but the harder it gets the less competition you have.

When was the last time you felt like nothing worse could happen to you, and what was it that made you feel that way?

_____
_____
_____

What happened afterwards? How did you solve the problem?

_____
_____
_____

Was the problem really as big as you thought it was?

_____
_____
_____

STOP CRYING! GET UP AND TAKE ACTION

Have you ever been in a situation where you were about to give up because everything looked bad, but then things changed and everything came out as expected, and then you asked yourself, what if I didn't try one more time? ____ Yes ____ No. What was it?

_____
_____
_____

What did you learn from the story of the castaway?

_____
_____
_____

How are you going to apply the lesson learned from the story to the challenges you are facing at this moment?

_____
_____
_____

In which stage of success are you at this moment?

Be _____

Do _____

Have _____

Chapter 9: Your Image Is Important

&

"THE COWL DOESN'T MAKE THE MONK." Have you ever heard that saying? Although it's true, the reality is that people do judge you and treat you based on how you look.

When I was working as a truck driver, I went to make a delivery in the city of Anaheim, California. When I arrived to the building where I had to make the delivery, I found that the cargo elevator was out of service, so I had to use the general elevator. Most of the people who work in that building are business people, so most of them had business attire.

When I got to the elevator, there were a few people waiting for it, but when the door opened one of the people extended his arm, signaling me to go ahead. I proceeded to get into the elevator with my load. Nobody else followed me in; the people let me ride the elevator by myself. My first thought was that these people did not get in the elevator with me because they thought they were too good to ride the elevator along with a truck driver.

Later I understood that the people who did not want to get in the elevator with me were not necessarily rude. I understood that someone who is dressed neatly may not want to be near someone who is not well-dressed. I was all sweaty; in addition to that, I was carrying dusty boxes. After all, who wants to be close to someone who is dirty? Nobody! Right?

Some years later, I had to go to the city of Anaheim again, but this time I was well-dressed, and when I got to the elevator, I found other people waiting for it, too. When the door opened one of the people there extended his arm, signaling me to go ahead. I was thinking, "Here we go again; they're going to let me ride the elevator all by myself."

Surprisingly, once I got in the elevator, the other people got in it, too, and we all went up.

I was amazed and I asked myself, "Why did people change towards me and treated me better this time?" What happened was that the people in Anaheim had not changed, but I had. The first time I went there, I was dressed differently; I was dressed according to the job I had. The second time, things were different. I was now well-dressed and the people at the elevator felt I was at their level, so I got the respect I deserved.

You might think, "Well, but people should treat everyone the same." It's true. That's how it *should be*, but when it comes to what *is*, things aren't like that; but, at the same time, it's understandable.

During some of my presentations, I love to demonstrate to the audience how we all judge others by the way they look, and I do the following:

I display a picture of a group of homeless people then I ask, "If you are parked on the street, and you see that one of the people in this group starts walking toward your car, what do you think that person is going to do?"

"Ask for money," everybody answers.

Then I show a picture of a group of well-dressed people and ask the audience again, "If you are parked on the street, and see that one of *these* people is walking toward your car, what is the first thing you think he or she is going to do?"

People's response is, "He or she is going to ask for help finding an address or about a nearby business."

Lastly, I show a picture where there is a group of gang members making their signs and showing their tattoos, and I ask the audience, "If you are parked on the same place and you see one of these guys walking towards your car, what do you think he is going to do?"

Normally, everyone in the room yells, "I'd better take off, because most likely he is going to try to either steal my car or rob me."

You see? We all judge each other by the way we dress.

If you dress nicely, other people will treat you nicely, because they don't know who you are; all they know is that you look like a decent person. They might be wrong, but that's how you look and that's what you represent to them.

I'd like to invite you to take a challenge. Dress with regular clothes and visit a restaurant or business close to your house where they don't know you. Then, go back to that same place a couple of days later, but this time dress differently. Dress professionally. I guarantee you that you'll notice the difference.

No matter where you go, your image is important. Dress sharply all the time, because you never know when or where you could meet a person who could help you change your life; people are judging you all the time, and one of the first things people see about you is the way you dress.

The way you dress says a lot about you.

Usually people dress based on how they feel. A depressed person or someone with low self-esteem tends to neglect him/herself; therefore, they don't care whether they look good or not. But when you feel great you dress neatly, because you understand people are always judging, and you want to make a good impression.

When I was a car salesman there was a guy named Mario. Mario was overweight. I think that was a big problem for him; his self-esteem was very low, and he was always dressing scruffy. He was always wearing shirts that were stained and too small for him, and most of the time his shirt was not tucked in, and his belt was not properly buckled; his tie was all twisted, too.

Remember that I said people are always judging? The impression Mario was giving his clients was not the best it could be.

At that same car dealer, there was a young guy named Greg. Greg was the opposite of Mario; he always dressed sharply, and was always happy and talking to everyone.

Who do you think the clients felt better talking to, Mario or Greg? Greg, of course! Nobody likes to talk to a person who looks bad.

People will treat you based on how you look, whether it is right or not; it's just human nature, and we all do it.

Although you always hear people saying not to judge a book by its cover, it's very hard to avoid judging people based on their appearance. If you're in sales, you know what I'm talking about.

A salesperson usually determines if he or she has a good client by judging how the client is dressed.

One of the best lessons I received regarding the judging of people by the way they dress was when I was in the car industry.

After patiently waiting for my turn to talk to the next walk-in prospect, a family in a very old, small truck arrived at the lot. My first thought was, "Great! I have just wasted my turn with these people; by the truck they're driving, I'm sure they don't qualify for anything." It wasn't only the fact that they were driving a piece of junk, but when they got out of the truck, the three of them looked very dirty. I shook their hand out of sheer courtesy, but in reality I didn't even want to do that.

After I welcomed them, they went straight to the best truck we had in the lot. One of the guys said, "This truck is very nice. I like it." My response was, "You're right. This is the nicest truck we have in the lot, but tell me how you're planning to buy, cash or credit?" I have to admit I was being sarcastic.

"I want to finance it," the guy said.

"Have you bought a car before?" I asked him.

"No," he said.

"Well, if that's the case, you need about a 30% down payment to buy this car. How much money do you have?" I asked him.

"I have one thousand dollars," he answered.

"You cannot buy this car with only one thousand dollars; you need a lot more than that, or get a co-signer."

"That's why I brought my mom with me, she'll co-sign for me," he said. I honestly wanted to laugh, because these people looked homeless. *This guy has to be kidding me*, I thought to myself; but he wasn't. He was serious.

"Do you have any credit ma'am?" I asked the lady.

"No," she said. *Just what I expected*, I thought to myself. The lady continued, "The only thing I am paying with credit is my house."

That changed everything, because whoever has a house qualifies to buy a car. Right then and there, I knew I had a good client, so I took them in the office. The manager ran the lady's credit. Her credit was excellent and she could buy the car they wanted with only one thousand dollars down. What I learned from that experience was that I can never judge people by the way they look.

Do you think your image matters and, if so, why?

_____
_____
_____

Have you ever felt like you were mistreated just because of the way you looked?

_____
_____
_____

Have you ever judged someone else without knowing that person just by the way he or she was dressed?

_____
_____
_____

How were you treated when you visited the business or restaurant wearing regular clothes?

_____
_____
_____

How were you treated the second time you visited the same establishment, but well-dressed?

_____
_____
_____

How are you going to dress from now on?

_____

_____

Next time you see someone on the street or anywhere else dressed in a certain way, are you going to judge that person just by the way he or she looks?

_____

_____

_____

Chapter 10: Train Your Mind for Success

WE ALL WENT THROUGH A CERTAIN TRAINING to get to think the way we think today, and our thoughts have taken us to where we are today. We're the result of the actions we've taken repeatedly over the years.

We can condition our mind to achieve anything we want to achieve in life. All we have to do is to determine what we want.

For example, a person who decides to become a professional boxer, starts training not only his body, but also his mind. The training will condition his mind and his body to withstand the punches he'll receive from his opponents in each fight.

Just like the professional boxer, if you want to be successful you must train yourself and your mind for that purpose.

The main reason it's so difficult to change our way of thinking and our beliefs is that we've been thinking the same way our whole life. We were conditioned to believe certain things, and it's very difficult to change something that has been with us for so many years.

Our thoughts and beliefs are going to take us where we want to go. Those same beliefs can make us stay where we are today—or, even worse, they can make us go back.

What can we do to get better results, if we're not satisfied with the results we're getting today?

As children, we were trained by our parents, our family members and our religious leaders, just to name a few. Now that we're grownups, we're responsible of our actions and results; we have to retrain our minds.

For that we can hire a professional trainer. A trainer can help us accelerate our results and achieve our goals.

You may have noticed that all professional sports players have a trainer or coach. A coach can help you identify your limitations, and work in those specific areas to recondition your mind so you can get the results you're looking for.

One of the things I've learned is that *reality* doesn't exist. Each person creates their own reality. In the beginning, this wasn't easy for me to understand, because I used to think *reality* was just that, reality. But it isn't always like that. *You* are the one who decides how to interpret what happens in your life.

In 2013, I was appointed to be one of the contestants for the Humorous Contest in the Toastmasters club I belonged to. I like challenges, so I accepted, knowing that I was not a very funny person. The date of the competition was fast approaching, and I still didn't have anything prepared. I had no idea what I could talk about that would be funny enough to make people laugh. Humor wasn't my thing.

I was in a debate with myself as to whether I should participate. I was about to call and cancel my participation. During those days I was reading Tony Robbins' book *Awaken the Giant Within*. In that book, Tony says that reality doesn't exist, and that *you* are the one who interprets life and situations however you want to see them.

So, what I did was to turn a "sad story" into a funny story. I ended up winning the 1st place in the club, and 2nd place in the area, just because I learned how to turn something negative into something funny and positive.

One of the best ways to train your mind for success is reading books. Books provide lots of information, and can arm you with useful tools that can help you grow in the area you want to grow.

Another way to train your mind for success is reading biographies of people you admire. By doing that, you'll find a lot of interesting stories of people who were or are just like you, and achieved big things in life after they trained their mind for success.

One of the biographies that impacted my life was the one about Jim Rohn. Jim was totally broke; and when I say *broke*, I mean *BROKE*. As he tells the story, his life changed when he had to lie to a Girl Scout, because he couldn't even afford to buy a chocolate from her. Jim died a millionaire, and he got to be one of the best coaches in history. His legacy will prevail forever. If you want to know more about Jim's story go to the internet, type his name, Jim Rohn, and you'll be able to read his entire story.

Everyone who has reached success has a story that is similar to Jim's story.

Train your mind for success; attend as many trainings as possible.

A person asked me once, "Moises, why do go to so many trainings? I see you everywhere." My answer was, "I go to a lot of trainings because I always learn something new in each one of them, and because you never know where you'll go where someone will say a word or a phrase that will literally change your life." I said that because that's exactly what happened to me. The phrase that changed my life was, "Success is something that is learned."

If you're looking for a change that hasn't happened yet, don't worry; it'll arrive. The good thing is that you're already looking for it, and when you're looking for something, you'll find it. Just be patient and *always* be alert so you can recognize the opportunity when it arrives.

KEEP YOUR MIND BUSY

Have you noticed that when your mind is not busy, that little voice we all have in our heads starts talking to you? Have you noticed that the busier you are the less you hear that little voice? Keep your mind busy and shut that little voice off once and for all.

You may have never paid attention to the fact that when you are not doing anything that voice starts talking to you. Let's do an experiment, stop reading after this sentence and try not to do anything for a minute.

Isn't it true that, once you stopped reading, that little voice started talking to you?

For some reason, that voice never has good things to say; it seems as if its job would be to torture you. The good news is that you can control that voice whenever you want to.

Your mind can only do one thing at the time; therefore, if you keep your mind busy, there'd be no time for that voice to talk to you. The less attention you pay to that voice, the better.

One of the best ways to avoid listening to the little voice is to keep your mind busy, either reading a book, listening to a motivational audio, or investing your time in creating something new. All these things require all of your attention and concentration, so there would be no time or room for anything else in your head.

A person who suffers from depression tends to isolate him/herself from the rest of the people; they like to be alone for long periods of time.

During the time these people are alone, they don't even think. All they do is listen to their inner voice and, sadly, like I said before, that voice doesn't have anything good to say, so the only thing that's happening is that the person is torturing him/herself, because he/she is not controlling his/her thoughts.

How do I know that?

Because I was there; I suffered from depression for years. I know how it feels to be depressed. One of the things I used to do was to stay away from the crowds; I could not stand being close to other people.

Now that you know that most of your problems come from your own head, it's time to take control of your thoughts and actions. Determine what you want to accomplish. Start making a plan to get to where you want to go. Keep your mind as busy as possible.

One of the decisions I have to make every time I get in my car is, should I listen to the regular radio or should I listen to something that is going to keep me interested and keep my mind busy?

The difference between listening to a regular radio station and listening to an audio you are interested in, is that your mind already knows the songs and commercials that will play in the radio; therefore, your mind can be listening to the radio and talking trash to you at the same time.

Think about something you need to learn, something that is related to one of your goals. Buy an audio and a book, so that whether you're driving somewhere or waiting for an appointment you can keep your mind busy.

Now that I am aware, I see a lot of people how look frustrated. When they're driving in rush hour traffic, or waiting impatiently in line or for an appointment, I see them and tell myself, "Yup! That was me a few years ago."

Now, I simply listen to audio programs that interest me, which contain information that will keep my mind alert.

When you're listening to something that interests you, you have to:

1. Pay attention to what you're listening to,
2. Absorb and assimilate the information,
3. While you're listening or reading the information, your brain is working to determine in what area of your life you can apply what you're learning.

The beauty of this is that once you start listening to audio programs and reading books, your mind becomes hungry for information.

Your mind is like a muscle; the more you work it the bigger it becomes; the bigger it is, the more information you need to fill the empty spot.

As with any other thing in life, if you want to be successful you have to train your mind for success.

The only way you're going to train your mind for success is if:

- You read the right books
- You listen to the right information
- You hang around with successful people, and
- You never stop learning

Get your eyes used to seeing good things and your ears used to hearing good information, because that's what will train your mind for success.

What are you good at? What is your mind trained for?

_____

_____

What are you going to start doing to train your mind for success?

_____

_____

_____

Who trained you as a kid? Is the training you received helping you or holding you back?

_____

_____

_____

What does your little voice tell you most of the time?

_____

_____

_____

What are you going to do to keep your mind busy and stop listening to your biggest enemy, your little voice?

_____

_____

_____

Name five successful people that you're interested in knowing more about (to read their biographies).

_____

_____

_____

Of the biographies you have read, name three people that you will remember every time you feel like giving up.

_____
_____
_____

CHAPTER 11: HAVE FAITH

AT THE BEGINNING OF YOUR JOURNEY you will need a lot of strength, a lot of courage, and a lot of character because there will be times when you'll feel like giving up.

One of the main reasons people don't reach success is because they don't have enough faith. Their faith is so weak that almost anyone can kill their dreams.

In order for you to be successful you'll need a lot of courage to accomplish what you started. You'll need a lot of character to not listen to people who tell you not to do it because you could fail. And lastly, you'll need the guts to face the naysayers and start over every time you fail. You cannot let anyone discourage you or make you doubt yourself.

Faith is something that not everybody has. Everybody talks about it, but only a few know the real meaning of it. Faith is to be able to see the invisible and be able to touch the intangible. That's why people around you think you're crazy. That's right; they call you crazy because they cannot see what you see.

One of the phrases that impacted me was a phrase a speaker said in one of the trainings I attended. He said, "Five hundred people confirmed their attendance to this event. I prepared the room for only two hundred fifty because I already know half of the world gives up even before they start."

But why is this? Because people do not have commitment. People want results but they aren't willing to go through the process. Everybody wants to harvest but only a few are willing to till the soil and sow the seed.

Everything is more difficult at the beginning because you start with nothing. Things are not visible yet, and most people believe in the saying "Seeing is believing." Well, I have a message for you, it's the opposite, "You need to believe if you want to see."

I see success like the difference between the flight of an airplane from Laredo, Texas to Los Angeles, and vice versa.

An airplane that flies from Laredo to Los Angeles takes about thirty minutes more than the flight from Los Angeles to Laredo. Why? Because when the airplane flies from Laredo to Los Angeles it's going against the wind currents; therefore, the airplane engines have to use more power and consume more fuel. But when it flies from Los Angeles to Laredo, the winds are in its favor and it takes the airplane 30 minutes less. Not only that, it also uses less fuel and its engines don't need to use all their power, because the wind is literally pushing the airplane.

Life is like that. In the beginning, it will be as if you're going from Laredo to Los Angeles, and the winds you're going to have to face will be your loved ones and your in-laws. They're going to tell you that you are crazy, to get a real job, to stop dreaming, and to put your feet on the ground.

Once you start doing something new, don't expect to see immediate results; but don't think about giving up, either, because you never know how close you could be from achieving your goal. Ritu Ghatourey said, "Don't stop because you're tired. Keep going because you're almost there." You could think, "Well, I work and work, and I don't see anything happening or changing in my life." Sometimes your personal growth is so imperceptible that not even *you* can notice it.

If people try to discourage you, don't take it personally, just keep on going. People are going to tell you things like, "You've been trying the same thing for years now and I don't see you have gotten any results, why don't you just try doing something else?" Never listen to those people; personal growth is something that is not visible to others, because it's happening *internally*, just like it happens with the Japanese bamboo.

The Japanese bamboo is a plant that doesn't grow immediately. A few days after the bamboo seed is planted, a small plant comes out of the soil and grows just a little bit. The plant stays about the same size, not for one year, not for two or three years, but for seven years! That's right; the bamboo plant apparently doesn't grow at all for seven years. All of a sudden, in a period of only six weeks the plant that apparently didn't grow for seven years reaches a height of 30 meters, in some cases. During the time of apparent inactivity, what the plant was doing was that it was working hard developing a complex system of roots that was going to help it support the sudden growth. Everything happens underground, where nobody can see. All the changes occur where people can't see what's going on; that's why people question what you do.

I can tell you that most of the people around me—including my mother-in-law, my Mom, my Dad, my brothers and friends—criticized me when I was at the beginning of my journey. The only one who always trusted me was my wife, Jackie. No matter what I would do she always supported me, but besides her nobody would give me the time of day. And, you know what? In a way, they (the people around me) were right, because there was no way I could show them what I was seeing.

Eventually, most of the people who criticized me in the past called me to ask for some kind of help and to tell me that they always knew I could do it. It sounds funny today, but at that moment, it was not; especially because I was in need of help and nobody was there for me, except for my brothers and my wife.

Although my brothers did not agree with what I was doing, they helped me with money so I could pay my rent and my bills, and buy food.

I have a saying, "If nobody has called you crazy yet, it's because you have not started on your road to success."

If people call you crazy, if nobody believes in you, and if everybody criticizes you, you are going in the right direction.

One of my uncles once told me, "You know what, nephew? I admire you for your patience; you don't stop, not even when things don't work out right." I told him, "Uncle, what I have isn't patience; what I have is faith. I don't know how long it's going to take for me to get to where I want to be; all I know is that I will get there one day."

The reason I think this way is because there is a paragraph in the book The God Memorandum, by Og Mandino, that says, "The greater the payment is withheld, the better it will be for you... and compound in compound interest is the biggest benefit." This helps me to continue every day.

When I read that phrase, I told myself, "Man, when I receive my payment it's going to be a fortune."

Be ready to face the strong winds; work on yourself as much as you can. If things don't look good, don't worry; your payment has just been put on hold, for now. But when your time comes, it will be just like the Japanese bamboo. You'll grow so fast that people will be amazed, and you'll see the rewards of your work.

Let me give you another example of faith. It's 12:00 noon. You don't see the sun because it's cloudy. Even though you don't see the sun, you know it's up there. You have no doubt about it because it's 12:00 noon. Success is exactly the same; there will be times when you won't be able to see your objective, but that's OK. All you have to know is that it's there.

Have you started something and abandoned it because of lack of faith?

_____

_____

Have you abandoned a project because others discouraged you? If so, what was it?

_____

_____

_____

What do you commit yourself to today?

_____

_____

_____

What are you going to do when everybody turns their backs on you, are you going to give up or are you going to continue?

_____

_____

_____

Are you willing to face the strong winds?

_____

What are you going to do if you fail?

_____

_____

_____

What did you learn from the story of the Japanese bamboo?

_____

_____

_____

Do you have the character and the courage strong enough to face all the obstacles that life will present to you?

_____

_____

_____

Chapter 12: Become a Person of Good Habits

❧

SUCCESSFUL PEOPLE HAVE SOMETHING IN COMMON: They all have good habits. A person with good habits is a reliable person and earns the respect of others. Acquiring good habits is essential on the road to success.

ALWAYS BE ON TIME

The other day I had a presentation. The attendees were told to be there at 7:00 PM. It was 7:15, and only a couple of people had arrived. Among them, there was a lady who was a leader of a network marketing company. She was very upset and asked why they had told her to be there at 7:00, if the training was not going to start on time. She said that, in her organization, one of the rules was to start the meeting at the established time, whether there was one person or a hundred. The organizer tried to explain to her that the reason they told people to be there at seven was because most people don't show on time.

Although the lady was right, the reality is that a very high percentage of people have the bad habit of arriving late. That's why most of the people who organize events set the meeting time thirty minutes to an hour before the event will actually start. That's basically for events that are open to the public. But if you have your own company or if you are the leader of your group, you can set your own rules and be stricter, which I think is a good idea because the only way people will succeed is if they are disciplined in all areas of their lives.

In 2001, I joined a network marketing company. That is actually the company to which I owe my change of mindset. One of the areas where they were very strict was about being on time. What they would do was to let everybody know doors will be closed right at 7:00, and nobody else would be allowed to enter even a second after that.

That was a rule everybody in the company knew, and more than once I saw people knocking at the door asking to be let in. The answer they received was, "You're late; there are no exceptions here, so please be here on time next week."

Some people disagreed with that rule and gave a list of reasons why they could not be on time. The leader's response was, "This is your own business, and if you are serious about it you are going to do whatever it takes to be here on time. How come we can all be here on time, except you? We all have things to do and most of us have a busy life, but we make the time to be here because we are serious."

Was the rule extreme? Yes, it was; but only for the people who had the bad habit of getting there late. For the people who were disciplined, that rule was just perfect.

DO NOT PROCASTINATE

Procrastination is another bad habit that affects a lot of people, and I am guilty of that. I think we all suffer from the same problem. The good thing is that once you are conscious of it, you can fight the problem. When I was asked by my manager how was I doing with this book, I told him I was going to have it ready in thirty days. The days were going by, and although, in reality, I was really busy because I had acquired a responsibility that was demanding most of my time, sometimes I *did* have a chance to write, but I would tell myself, *"I'll do it tomorrow."* But the next day I was just as busy as the day before, so at the end of the day I had still not written anything, and again I would tell myself the same thing. The days went by like this, and the date I had given my Manager to have my book finished, arrived.

On that very day, I sent my Manager a message to let him know that I had not finished the book, yet, and that I would have it finished no later than six weeks from that date. Today is Sunday, and after going out with the family for a little bit, here I am, still writing. It's 9:24 PM, but I cannot stop. I have to finish the book by the agreed upon date.

What I'm doing now is the opposite of what I did before, which didn't work. Before, every time I had a chance to write I would tell myself, "I will do it tomorrow." Now, every time I have a chance to write I tell myself, "I'm going to write right now that I have a little bit of time, because I don't know if tomorrow I will have time to do it." This way, I have already written about eight pages today.

When you are aware of what you're doing right or wrong, it's easier to overcome that problem.

HONOR YOUR WORD

If people don't achieve success, it's just because most don't do what they say they were going to do. They lie to themselves.

Hundreds of years ago, and even perhaps a few decades ago still, people didn't need contracts to make deals. All they needed to do to consider a deal closed was just a handshake and their word. If someone sold a cow to someone else for a certain price and a minute later another person offered more money for the same cow the owner of the cow would say, "I'm sorry, but I already gave my word to someone else and I cannot sell it to you." This was so, even when the person who had bought the cow hadn't paid for it, yet. Back in those days, someone's word had real value.

Nowadays, things are different.

Do you know anyone who told you one thing one day, and then changed his/her mind and simply said, "I don't remember telling you that."?

Nowadays, it's very difficult to find people who honor their word. But what other people do is none of your business; what really matters is whether *you* are honoring *your own* word.

When you honor your word, you gain respect because people know you are a responsible person. More people want to do business with you when you are recognized as a man or a woman of your word.

SMILE

Smiling is one of the best habits you can develop, because who wants to be near a person who looks very serious, sour or almost angry? No one, right?

But if you're someone who is always smiling and looks happy, people will want to be close to you. Nobody can reject a nice smile. Don't believe me? Try it. Today when you are out there, smile to a stranger and see what happens. I guarantee you that one of two things will happen:

1. The person will look at you as if you're crazy, but will smile back at you. Probably a fake smile, but he or she will smile.
2. That person will smile back at you and may even ask you a question or try to start a conversation.

What is a great benefit of smiling all the time? You never know who you're smiling at. It may be a potential client for your business or maybe that person knows someone who could help you reach your goal.

ALWAYS TALK POSITIVELY

Have you ever been in a place where someone approaches you and, after introducing him/herself, he/she starts talking about all the negative things in the world? Those people talk like that because that's their world; that's the reality they live in.

A few months ago, I was talking to a person who had lots of information regarding the economy, inflation, and unemployment; he even showed me facts and figures.

This person was an expert in all the negative things you can imagine. He was one hundred percent concentrated on the negative.

Make sure you are not that type of person, and that the words that come out of your mouth are positive words, words of hope, and your words have to encourage others. The only way you're going to get to where you want to go is by having a good attitude.

If you are not a positive person or if you consider that you still have things to work on, don't worry; today is a good day to start to change, because it is possible to change.

In this chapter I talked about someone else being negative and being an expert in negative things. Many years ago I was just like that person. My life was full of negativity and everything seemed to be impossible for me. I was hopeless and depressed.

One of the things I tell people in my presentations is that a few years ago none of them would have wanted to be close to me. Everybody asks, "Why not?" I reply, "Because a few years ago I was the exact opposite of who I am today. I was very negative; I was always mad, and I would blame the system, the people around me and even the weather for my situation." Most of the time, people in the audience say something along the lines of, "It's very difficult for me to imagine you being like that." But that's the truth. This just proves that, if I can change, anybody can change.

The change in my attitude had to do with the fact that I learned success is something that is learned, so I decided to start learning how to be successful.

You might not be successful today, but that doesn't mean you cannot be successful in the future. Just make sure you start taking action, or else nothing will happen.

How many bad habits do you have? Write them here:

_____

_____

_____

How good are you at being on time? And, if you are not, what are you going to do to change that habit?

_____

_____

_____

Are you a procrastinator? If so, what is it that you have been leaving for tomorrow but you are now going to take immediate action on?

_____

_____

_____

Do you honor your word most of the time or just some times?

_____

_____

What action are you going to take to change the habit of not honoring your word?

_____

_____

_____

Have you caught yourself talking negatively? If so, what are you going to do to change that?

_____
_____
_____

There is nothing more powerful than beliefs.

Do you believe you can achieve whatever you want and that everything is possible in this life if you take the necessary steps to make things happen?

_____
_____
_____

Chapter 13: The Price of Success

◈

"Life has knocked me down a few times. It has shown me things I never wanted to see. I have experienced sadness and failures. But one thing is for sure…. I always get up." - Unknown

THE NICE THING ABOUT SUCCESS IS THAT IT HAS A HIGH PRICE, and not everybody is willing to pay it.

Have you ever bought something from a vending machine? What happens if you don't deposit the right amount or more, to purchase the product you want to buy? The vending machine simply doesn't release the product, right? Can you negotiate with a vending machine? No, you can't.

Success is exactly like that vending machine; it will not release the product to you until you have paid the right amount or more for what you want. The price you'll have to pay will depend on what you want to achieve. Some people will feel successful making $3,000 a month, but others won't feel successful unless they're making at least $100,000 per month. The universe is infinite and there are options for everyone, and *you* are the one who decides how much you want. Do you want a little or you want a lot? You'll end up getting only what you ask for.

On the road to success, you'll find a lot of obstacles, like the quote at the beginning of this chapter says, "Life is going to knock you down." For some unknown reason, all the people who have achieved big things first had to go through a process; that's what I call *preparation*.

When you're looking for success, life will place you in situations you'd never thought would happen to you. There are two events in my life that I'd never thought would happen to me.

The first one is:

I NEVER THOUGHT I WOULD RUN OUT OF GAS IN MY CAR.

Whenever I'd see someone putting gas in their car on the side of the freeway or the street, the first thought that came to me was, *"How is it even possible for a person to run out of gas; I cannot believe they don't have at least five bucks to get to where they are going."*

When you're not in the other person's shoes, it's very easy for you to criticize.

During the crisis that started in 2008, my wife was the only one who had a stable job, and she was essentially the only one bringing money home, because in my job I was paid straight commissions, and would only get paid once in a while. One day, before she left for work, she asked me if the amount of gasoline she had in the truck was enough for her to get to work. I told her, "Yes, it is." Those days, we were trying to spend as little as possible; or rather, we didn't have anything to spend. We were actually short at the end of every month.

My wife left for work and she made it. The problem was in the afternoon, on the way home from work. As she was getting out of the parking lot, the truck stalled. She tried to start the engine again, but she couldn't. The truck had run out of gas. She called me to tell me what was happening, but I couldn't do anything because the only car we had was the truck she was driving. She ended up getting some help to move the truck on the curb, then she called one of her nephews, and asked him to pick me up to go help her.

My wife's nephew picked me up, but by this time my wife had already gone to the gas station; she bought a small container and a couple of bucks' worth of gasoline. She put the gasoline in the tank, but it wasn't enough; she couldn't get the truck started.

By the way, one of the reasons we had not put gasoline in the truck was because we only had a little over $10 in our bank account. So the plan was to pay for the gasoline with the ATM card, knowing our account was going to be overdrawn (This was a practice we learned while in the midst of the crisis) but, at least, we were going to have a full tank for one more week.

The other reason was that sometimes during the day I would make some money, but that wasn't the case on that particular day.

When my wife's nephew and I arrived to where my wife was we checked the truck and everything else was fine, so the only thing it needed to start was gasoline. I had brought a bigger container with me, so we went to the gas station and bought a little more gas. We went back to where my wife and the truck were, put the gas in the tank and the truck started. "Problem solved."

I put "Problem solved" in quotation marks because remember we only had a little more than $10 in our account? Well, with the purchase of the container and gasoline my wife bought the first time, the account was already overdrawn. Then I used the card again to buy a little more of gas. So, we already had two separate overdraft charges, and each overdraft penalty was $35.

We were embarrassed to let other people know we were broke, so we didn't ask my wife's nephew for financial help. We thanked him for helping us and he left.

My wife and I had another problem now. We didn't know if the card was going to go through one more time, and we didn't know whether the gas we had put in the truck already was going to be enough for us to make it home. We had no choice, so we went to the gas station one more time. I remember handing the ATM card to the cashier. I drew a smile on my face, but at the same time I was praying for the card to go through.

Surprise! The ATM did *not* go through. I had to act as if nothing was wrong and asked the cashier, "Are you sure it didn't go through? Why don't you try it as a credit card, instead?" He tried one more time and… Bingo! This time it did go through. We filled the tank and went home. "Problem solved!"

Problem solved? Now we had a bigger problem, because we had no money at all. We were overdrawn in our bank account, because we used the ATM card *three times*. This meant $35 X 3 = $105 just in overdraft charges.

That experience helped me to understand why people run out of gas. It was very clear to me now. The reason people don't put gasoline in their cars is because they are just like I was at that time: BROKE!

The second thing I never thought would happen to me:

I was in a situation where I had to pay my rent, my car insurance, my life insurance, and buy food for my family. I needed about two thousand dollars to cover all of these expenses. What was the problem? The problem was that I didn't have a single dollar in my pocket, and I was forced to do what I consider one of the worst things I have ever done in my life, *lie*. I had to lie to get money.

I called one of my clients, who was a business owner. I knew he had money, and I also knew he trusted me; so I called him and told him I was starting a project but I was going to need more money than I had anticipated. He asked me how much I needed, "Five thousand dollars," I said.

He thought for a second and told me, "I can lend you three thousand."

"That's OK," I said. "I promise to pay the money back in about six months."

When I hung up, I asked myself, "How much lower can I go? I'm lying to get money; I'm betraying someone who trusts me." Then I thought, "It's either that or my family and I end up on the street and without food." I felt so bad because I was not being me; I was doing something that was totally against my principles.

Eventually, I paid the three thousand dollars back, but it took me a few years to do that.

I had never been so bad, financially speaking; but, at the same time, I had never been so sure that one day I was going to become a successful person. I knew that what was happening was that I was starting to pay the price of success; and although life had knocked me down, the fight was not over, yet.

As you can see, the price of success is high and you have to be willing to pay it, if you really want it.

Along the road, success will show you things you never wanted to see; things like seeing your family suffer along with you. There will be sadness in you, when you find yourself alone fighting to get out of the hole you're in. You'll feel so bad when you see there is nobody there for you. You'll have to face the difficult times on your own, because when you are down nobody wants to know about you, and nobody wants to be close to you. The only thing your family and friends will do will be to criticize what you are doing and give their opinion about what should you do.

Perhaps one of the most difficult situations you have to face when you are looking for success will be when you start a new project. Usually at that stage you're all excited, and you share your idea with the people you love. Your friends and family will listen to you, but at the same time they'll think you're crazy.

You have to prepare yourself mentally in case you fail, because people will come to you and tell you, "See? I told you so. You're dreaming; you have to be realistic. Get a *real* job and stop doing things that don't work." When you try something and fail, the people around you will make you feel like you are worthless and stupid. They make you feel like a real failure. Be careful of situations like that because you'll doubt yourself many times. Build a shell and, if you fail, get up and try one more time. You're allowed to fail, but you're not allowed to give up.

Are you willing to pay the right price for success? If so, why would you do that? What will be the benefit of doing that?

_____

_____

_____

Have you already faced a situation in your life that you never thought you were going to have to face? What was it?

_____

_____

_____

Have you ever been without any money in your pocket?

_____

_____

_____

What has been the lowest thing you have done to get money? (If you have done something like that).

_____

_____

_____

In your search for success, what have you seen that you didn't like or wanted to see in your life?

_____

_____

_____

You may be going through a difficult situation today, but how determined are you to fight for what you want and reach success?

_____

_____

_____

Write what you're going to do to reach success and how determined you are to achieve what you want.

_____

_____

_____

Chapter 14: The First Steps Are Always the Hardest

Fear, uncertainty and insecurity are three of the main reasons why people don't dare to take action. Most people are waiting for the planets to be aligned and lady luck to be in their favor, so they can take the first step. This happens mainly because people are afraid to fail and they don't want to do anything unless it is 100% guaranteed. In real life, there is no such thing as *guaranteed* or *for sure*; everything involves risks and if you are not willing to take risks you'll never have a chance to win.

In 1976 Ronald Wayne sold his 10% stake in Apple for only $800. At the time I'm writing this chapter, Apple, Inc. is worth $58,065,210,000. What happened? Why did Ronald sell his shares? He sold his shares because he didn't want to take any risks and because he never thought the company was going to be worth what it's worth today.

If you're asking yourself whether you should take action or not, stop thinking about it and take action today. Think less and do more. Actions provide better results than mere thoughts. The best way to make things happen is by taking the first step.

YOU DON'T WAIT FOR THE CONDITIONS TO GET BETTER IN ORDER TO START; THE CONDITIONS WILL GET BETTER ONCE YOU START.

I'm writing this in the month of October; we're *almost* at the end of the year but I hear a lot of people say they're going to wait until *next year* to start working on their projects because the year is already over. Really? We still have about ninety days left. There is a lot that can be done in the next ninety days.

It is said that "The longer you wait the harder it gets." I really like this phrase because it's very true. Have you ever told someone you were going to call him/her but you didn't right away? As time passes, it gets harder and harder for you to call that person, right?

It's the same in all aspects of life, the longer you wait the harder it gets.

If you say you're going to do something but you let time go by and don't do it, as more time goes by it becomes harder for you to take action. In order to avoid that, you have to apply the six-hour rule.

The six-hour rule says that, once you make a decision, it's important that you take action in the next six hours, or else you might end up abandoning that idea, just like you've abandoned hundreds of ideas throughout your life.

Most of the time, things are not as difficult or as scary as we think they are.

I was twenty-two years old when I went to Six Flags® Magic Mountain for the first time. I was not a big fan of those types of amusement parks, mainly because I was afraid of the big rides; but my wife, Jackie (who was my girlfriend at the time), asked me if I wanted to go. I had to prove to Jackie just how brave I was, so I agreed and we went.

Back in those days the biggest ride Magic Mountain had was *Superman the Ride* ™. To start off, we didn't get on the big rides, and although I was scared of the rides we *did* get on, I was thinking, *OK. This is cool; these rides are not too high.* But no matter in which section of the park we were, we could hear the loud roar the *Superman* ride was making. I was scared to death and, deep inside, I was thinking, *I hope Jackie doesn't ask me to get on that thing.* Sure enough, sooner than I thought, I was facing the moment I was dreading. Jackie asked me, "Do you want to get on the *Superman* ride, or are you afraid?" In the depths of me, I was afraid to the core; but I couldn't show it or let her know how afraid I was, so I said, "Sure, why not!"

We stood in line and, while we were snaking around the stanchions, I was pretending everything was fine. Deep inside I was wishing for Jackie to say she didn't want to get on it; but my saving grace did not happen.

As we were getting closer and closer to the station to get in the cars, I felt my heart pumping harder and harder, and I wanted to get out, but I couldn't do that. I couldn't look like a coward in front of my girlfriend. Almost to the end of the line, right before getting on the ride, there was a sign advising people that they still had time to get out if they weren't sure they wanted to continue. Right there, I pointed to the sign and asked my girlfriend, "Are you sure you want to do this?"

"Yes," she said. "You're not sure, are you? Are *you* scared?" she asked.

"Of course not! I'm saying it for you," I told her.

The truth is I wanted to get out, but I had no choice. The roar of the cars going up and down made my fear grow even more. When it was our turn, we sat entered one of the cars. The security bar made the definitive noise: Click.

Right at that moment I knew there was nothing else to do, but enjoy the ride. The next thing I knew, we were holding on tight in that car going up a hundred miles an hour, in the ride that was more than four hundred feet high. Then, something interesting happened. When we were all the way up there I didn't feel fear anymore. My fear had magically disappeared, and turned into exhilaration. I was now *enjoying* the ride. Suddenly, the car started going in reverse. In less than ten seconds we were back to the starting point. With the adrenaline at 100%, the fear was not there anymore, and all I wanted to do was to experience that rush again.

As I said before, most of the time things aren't as difficult or scary as we think they are.

LIFE IS NOT EASY

I'm sure you've heard that phrase before, and it's true. Life is not easy; but it's also true that, most of the time, life is not as hard as we think it is, either.

No matter what you want to do, take that first step. Don't wait for the conditions to get better; take action and improve on the conditions. The first few steps are always the hardest, but in order for you arrive at your destination you must start walking now!

What have you tried to do, but you haven't started because you are afraid of that first step?

_____

_____

_____

Name a few things that you haven't done because you've let too much time pass, and as a result you ended up abandoning your idea:

_____

_____

_____

Are you the type of person who takes risks or do you like to play it safe?

_____

_____

How important do you think it is to take risks if you want to become successful?

_____

_____

_____

What is the first thing you're going to do, where you can apply the six-hour rule?

_____

_____

_____

What were you terrified of doing, and after you did it you asked yourself, *'Why did I wait so long if it was not difficult at all?'*?

_____

_____

_____

How are you going to apply this chapter to your life? What changes are you going to make?

_____

_____

_____

Chapter 15: Make Success Your Priority

☙

"When is the next meeting?" Jennifer asked me. Jennifer is a Real Estate agent who wants to learn how to speak in public. She asked me when our next meeting would be, because she knows I'm part of a club that helps its members develop their public speaking skills. The club I'm in is part of the nonprofit organization Toastmasters International: www.toastmasters.org.

Now, Jennifer had asked me that same question several times before. After giving her all the information, including the date and time, she said she would go to our next meeting. When date of the meeting arrived, Jennifer did not. Every time she calls to ask about the next meeting, I tell her the same thing, "Make it a priority."

"Yes, yes," she says all the time. To this day, as I'm writing this book, Jennifer has yet to make it to a meeting.

In life there are priorities, and they change depending what's more important for you.

For most people, their number one priority is going to work so they can provide for their families. Let's say you're at work (your priority); your phone rings and the person on the other end of the line tells you something like, "I'm calling to inform you that your son/brother/father just had an accident; it's nothing serious but he is in the hospital and gave me your number to let you know." What's your priority now? Your family member, right? Your job has just become a second priority to you.

Priority: Something that is regarded as more important than other things.

Even though Jennifer says she wants to learn how to speak in public, by her actions I can tell that learning to speak in public is not one of her priorities.

One thing is for sure, if Jennifer doesn't take action and makes learning how to speak in public one of her priorities, she will never learn how to do it.

You will only learn what you're interested in learning, nothing else.

Success is different for everybody and you are the only one who can determine what success is for you. Once you determine what success is for you, you'll have to make a list of the things you're going to have to do and learn in order to achieve your goal.

Success requires that you:

1. Do something different
2. Sacrifice
3. Have determination
4. Possess the right mental attitude

In one of the trainings I gave, I mentioned how people can make more money if they're not happy with the amount of money they were making. I shared with the audience how people get paid for what they know, and not for what they do. If you know a little, you'll get paid a little; if you increase your knowledge, now you become more valuable because by learning something new you increased your value in the market.

I provided the audience a web site called www.salary.com, told them to go there, search for the career that would pay them what they wanted, and take immediate action towards their goal. It sounds simple, and it is. But most people are not willing to change. Most of the people who are struggling want a better life and to make more money than what they're making now, but they want to get paid better doing the exact same things they have been doing for years, and it doesn't work that way.

Do something different: Doing something in the same way over and over will give you the same results all the time. If you want different results you have to start doing something different.

The first time I heard this was from an MLM company recruiter. He asked me:

Recruiter: What do you do for living?

Me: I work as a truck driver.

Recruiter: You must be making good money there.

Me: No, not really.

Recruiter: Then, why are you working there?

Me: Because I have to work.

Recruiter: How long have you been working as a truck driver?

Me: One year.

Recruiter: How much longer are you thinking about doing that?

Me: I don't know; until something better comes along, I guess.

Recruiter: If you continue doing what you're doing, do you think you will retire rich?

Me: No.

Then the recruiter told me, "As long as you keep doing what you're doing, you'll continue getting what you're getting; if you want your life to change, *you* have to change first."

In that moment, I didn't really understand what he meant by what he had told me; but later I realized that he was right. I needed to change if I wanted to change my results. So I did.

Sacrifice: It's in this section of the road where most people give up. Nobody likes to find obstacles along the way. Everybody wants a nicely paved and smooth street to success; but the reality is, there is no success without sacrifice. When learning English became my priority, I had to wake up at 5:45 AM to get ready for work, then work for ten long hours, rush from work to get home, take a shower and get ready for my classes.

One of the biggest sacrifices I had to make to accomplish my goal was go to school hungry. While I was in class, my stomach growled. My classes ended at 9:00 PM; right after my class was finished I used to run to a restaurant that was right in front of the school and grabbed something to eat. I did this for almost three years.

Like I said, most people give up where the sacrifices start. I remember that there were over forty people in a single classroom. All of us had the same intention: to learn English. For some reason, at the beginning of almost anything people get all excited, make plans and "commit" themselves; but when reality hits and people start to see things were not as easy as they thought they would be, they simply give up. That was the case in that class. As the days and weeks went by, the group of students got smaller and smaller.

Almost three years later, I finished my course. And out of all the people I had met at the first level, only a few of them finished the course with me. I saw some of my former classmates later, and asked them what had happened, why they had stopped going to class. All of them gave me a list of reasons why they stopped going to class. One of those reasons was, "Because I didn't have time to eat, and I would be hungry during class."

Have determination: A very high percentage of people don't accomplish their goals because they are not determined. When you are determined to accomplish something, there is no room for failure.

Kids can teach us a lot about determination. When my oldest daughter, Alyssa, was about three years old, she put on a blouse but she couldn't buckle the buttons. Her hands were still small and she didn't have the strength necessary to buckle her blouse or, at least that's what I thought.

Trying to help her, I remember telling her, "Come on, let me help you because you can't do it." Her answer was, "Yes, I can."

I insisted, "Come on, let me help you because you can't do it." She said one more time, "Yes, I can." Then I got busy reading, and Alyssa disappeared for about fifteen minutes. I'd even forgotten about what she was trying to do. All of a sudden, she came up to me with her blouse already buckled and told me, "See? I told you I could do it." When she told me that I laughed, because one of the things I had taught Alyssa was to never give up. By telling her she couldn't do it, I was not been consistent with what I'd been trying to teach her. Luckily, she had the attitude to reject my "help." But not only that, she proved to herself and she proved to me what she was capable of.

You either use your determination to accomplish your goals, or you will use it to help others to accomplish theirs. Let me give you an example.

Let's suppose you find a job you don't know anything about. The first day, you'd feel lost because you have no idea of how to do things right, or even what are the right things to do. But if you want to keep your job, you'll have to be determined to learn. If you're going to have determination at something, you might as well have determination to accomplish your goal.

Possess the right mental attitude

"Nothing can stop a person with the right mental attitude from achieving his goal; nothing can help a person with the wrong mental attitude." ~Thomas Jefferson

Reality doesn't exist; each person gives the meaning to situations, based on their own mental attitude. What seems to be a problem for someone could be just *a situation to be solved* for another. While the first person is worried because everything looks bad, the second person is looking for a solution. Same situation; different perspective and reaction.

Make it a priority to develop the right mental attitude that is essential to being successful. You either attract or push people away, based on your mental attitude.

The only way to become successful is by making a priority of what really matters.

Before you go to sleep at night, make a plan for the next day; see what is most important and give priority to that. As the day goes by, put a check mark next to each of the things that you're completing. At the end of the day, you'll see that when you have a plan you can do more things in a shorter period of time.

People say they want to accomplish certain things, but they give priority to other things. In sales, trainings are very important in order to serve your clients better, but many sales agents give priority to other things, instead. A few days ago I was talking to a Real Estate agent, and she said she was going to go to one of my trainings. When the date of the training arrived, she did not show up. I called her to see what had happened, and she said, "Oh! What happened was that a client called me yesterday and told me he wanted to come to the office today, so I decided to come to my appointment. But it turned out to be a waste of time because my client didn't show up."

In this example, the agent gave priority to her client and put the training as a second priority. Ultimately, the client didn't show up, and she missed the training. If we take a closer look at this case, we'd find that the reason the client didn't show up was precisely because she needs training. A well-trained real estate agent would have told their client, "Mr. Client, I'd love to see you tomorrow at 10:00 AM, but tomorrow is our office training where we learn how to better service our clients. Is it OK if we set our appointment for the day after tomorrow at the same time?" Do not let *any* circumstance take you away from your priorities; your priorities are all the things that will get you closer to your goal.

What is success for you? What, exactly, do you want to achieve?

_____

_____

_____

Have you given priority to things that take you away from your goal?

_____

_____

_____

What are you going to set as priority number one today?

_____

_____

_____

What are you going to start doing differently?

_____

_____

_____

What are you willing to sacrifice to reach your success?

_____

_____

_____

How determined are you to finish what you are about to start, or what you've already started?

_____

_____

_____

Be honest. Do you think you have the right mental attitude, or do you think you still need to work on it?

_____

_____

_____

If your mental attitude is not the best, what actions are you going to take to change it?

_____

_____

_____

Chapter 16: You Will Never Make People Happy

&

SUCCESS IS DOING WHATEVER MAKES YOU HAPPY without worrying what people may think or say about you. No matter what you do, you'll never make anybody happy; that's just impossible. To illustrate this idea better, let me tell you a story.

Once upon a time, a man and his son decided to visit some relatives. In order for them to get to the town where their relatives lived, they had to pass by a few other small towns, and the only transportation they had was a donkey. So the man and his son got on the donkey and started their trip. A couple of hours later they were passing by the first town. Suddenly the man overheard someone whispering, "Look how those people are happily riding the poor donkey; how heartless are they." The man, after hearing the comment the person made, thought it would be a good idea to let his son ride the donkey alone, once they got to the next town. When they arrived at the next town, the man got off the donkey and let his son ride it by himself. As they were going through the town, the man overheard someone else whisper, "Look at that selfish boy riding on the donkey, while the old man is walking." So the man thought it would be a good idea for him to ride the donkey once they got to the next town, and let his son walk for a little bit.

Once they got to the next town, the man asked the boy to get off the donkey, and he mounted it. As they were going through the town the man heard someone say, "Look at that poor boy walking while his father is very happy riding the donkey." The heeded that comment, and told his son that once they got to the next town both would get off the donkey and walk together for a little. Once they got to the next town, the father got off the donkey, so they both started to walk. While they were walking the man heard someone say, "Look at that couple of dummies walking, when they could be riding the donkey."

The moral of the story is this: No matter what you do, you'll never make people happy. That's why I say, success is doing whatever makes you happy without worrying about what people may think or say about you.

Most people never even try to pursue their dreams because they are too afraid of other people's opinions.

This story reminds me of the time when I was selling shaved ice on the streets. One of the things I always used to do was ask my customers if there were any job openings at the companies they were working for. My "friends" used to tell me all the reasons why I was never going to find another job. Their words of encouragement were, "Forget about finding another job. You don't have experience at anything. You don't know anything. You don't even speak English. Who is going to want to hire you?" But, for some reason, I never listened to them and eight months later, a person who bought a corn from me helped me get my first job. Right then and there, I understood the importance of persistence and not listening to others.

What have you been putting on hold? What is your dream, your passion? What is it that makes you feel alive and gives meaning to your life? Don't wait any more and start building your future today. Today has to be the beginning of your road to success.

"You don't have to be great to start, but you have to start to be great." -Zig Ziglar

There is only one way to get good at something and that is *trying*. That's right, you have to try, fail, and try again. Try, fail and try again, until you become good at it. You cannot expect to make birdies on your first day playing golf.

If you want to achieve something you'd better start today; don't wait until you are great at it. If things don't work out the way you wished, don't worry. Try again; maybe next time the outcome will be better; if it's not, don't get discouraged and try one more time. Remember; the more you try the better you become.

One of the things that entrepreneurs have in common is that all of them tried many different things and failed miserably most of the time. Some of them failed not one or two times, but *hundreds of times* before becoming successful. Persistence is another thing that differentiates successful people from the rest. No matter how bad things could go, they never lose enthusiasm, and are always ready to start again every time they fail. In order to reach success, you must become a warrior and fight many battles. The challenge is that you never know how many battles you're going to have to fight before you conquer your objective. If you are very, very lucky, you'll probably have to fight just a single battle. But, if not, you'll probably have to fight hundreds or even thousands of battles.

There will be times when you'll feel like quitting; you'll think your friends and family were right when they told you not to try, because you were going to fail. If you quit, then your friends and family will be right because only failures quit; winners persist until their last breath. Even if you die trying, it'll be worth it. It's better to die trying and live a life with purpose than to be "alive" and just be waiting for the day of your death.

On your way to success, you'll find people who will laugh at you, people who will talk behind your back, people who will think you're crazy; and there will be times when even you'll agree with them. When you start thinking differently, you become abnormal to the rest of the world, but that's OK. Be as abnormal as possible because, as Steve Jobs is quoted as saying, "People who are crazy enough to think they can change the world, are the ones who do."

When you're doing what everybody else is doing, nobody comes to bother you. Why? Because you're just another one of them; you are "normal," just like everybody else. The minute you start thinking differently, all the people around you come to tell you that you are crazy and to stop dreaming. When you think differently than the rest of the people that are around you, they'll come to attack you because they are losing you. After all the struggle and difficulties you'll have to overcome, when you finally achieve your goals, they'll come to tell you that you were just lucky. Never get distracted by the naysayers, and always remember, no matter what you do you'll never make people happy.

"They laugh at me because I am different; I laugh at them because they are all the same." ~Kurt Cobain

One of the hardest stages of success is when—no matter what you do—everything, and I mean everything, you try goes wrong. It is during this time when most people quit. People quit because they cannot handle the pressure, and they don't want anybody to make fun of them.

The reason why people laugh at you is because they don't have vision; it's impossible for them to see what you are seeing. Every time people laugh at you because of what you are doing, remember the phrase above. *You* are *not* like everybody else; you are different from the majority; you belong to a small percentage of people who have discovered their real purpose in life. If you already know what you want and what you're capable of, consider yourself fortunate. Over 90% of the people who come to this planet will die sorely unaware of their real potential, and they'll never find a real purpose to live for.

Never listen to those who tell you that you cannot do something, and always remember this: People without dreams don't have the right to kill someone else's dream.

What are going to start doing today that is going to get you closer to your goal?

_____

_____

_____

What did you learn from the story of the man, his son and the donkey?

_____

_____

_____

Who has ever told you things that have affected your life?

_____

_____

_____

What is your dream, your passion? What makes you feel alive and gives meaning to your life?

_____

_____

_____

If you fail, what are you going to do?

_____

_____

_____

If you try something and fail, what are you going to do when your friends or family members tell you "See, I told you so"?

_____

_____

_____

What is your vision? What do you see that the rest of the people cannot see?

_____

_____

_____

Chapter 17: Use the Tools Properly

&

FAITH, CONFIDENCE, BELIEF, DETERMINATION, CONVICTION, ATTITUDE, CERTAINTY AND VISION ARE TOOLS we all have, but use incorrectly most of the time.

These are the tools we use to get our results, whether those results are good or bad. Understanding this concept and taking charge of your life is one of the hardest things there is on Earth.

By nature, human beings tend to blame others for their failures when, in reality, each of us is responsible for each and every one of our own actions, decisions and results.

As I said before, we all have the powerful tools mentioned above, but the problem is that we use them in the wrong way. As a result, we end up proving to ourselves that we are nothing but failures every time we try to do something to better our lives, but end up failing, as always.

Of course, this has a lot to do with the information we received from the people that were in charge of programming our minds. A good example of this is Mario.

Mario is a business owner, and he has always been an entrepreneur. Mario was the owner of a car dealership, and I used to work for him. Mario knew I was reading a book about personal development; one day we were having a conversation, and he asked me, "Why do you have to read those books and listen to audios to motivate yourself? I don't need any of those things to motivate myself. My motivation is my businesses and the money I make from them."

"That's great! Now, let me ask you a question," I told him.

"Yes," he said.

"How did you learn about this business?" I asked him.

"Well," he said. "My dad owned a business like this, and he taught me how to buy cars at the auctions for a good price. He was very good at it. Everything my dad touched turned to gold. He would sell things that we thought he was never going to sell; but he was so good that he always ended up getting the money he wanted for his things."

As we can see, Mario was absolutely right. He didn't need to read any motivational or personal development books to reach his goals, because he came from a family where owning a business is the most common thing. Just by listening to Mario talk about his dad, I could tell that he learned from his dad how to use his tools the right way.

Every time Mario bought a car, he did it with faith. He was confident that he had made a good decision to buy it. He was determined to make money with it. He was convinced that buying and selling cars was his passion. He had a winning attitude. He was certain that nothing could stop him. And he'd visualize himself buying more cars in the near future. Mario uses his tools to succeed.

HOW DO AVERAGE PEOPLE USE THESE TOOLS?

Average people use these same tools, but to achieve failure. That's right; these same tools can be used for both purposes, to fail or to succeed.

Let's take someone says something like, "Another year working for this company, and many more to come." Does this person have faith? Yes, he does. He's talking about something that hasn't happened yet, but he knows will happen. When someone says something like that, it's because they're not looking for anything new, so they already know where they're going to be next year, and the next, and the next.

Continuing with the previous example, we'll see that the person celebrating another anniversary at work is very confident. They will still be there next year. So, is the tool of *confidence* being applied? Yes, it is. They also have the determination to keep doing the same thing they've done for years, so they can stay in the same place. They also have conviction, because they convinced themselves that there is nothing better for them out there, or that they don't deserve anything better. The attitude of someone who is not happy at their job is a loser attitude most of the time. Have you ever been to a place where there's an employee at the entrance who welcomes you with a *"Welcome to..."* but with a long face? A person without hope is always certain that they will be a failure. Lastly, they visualize themselves old, tired and broke.

As you can see, the tools are the same; but when they're used in a different way they produce different results.

HOW CAN YOU PROPERLY APPLY THE TOOLS YOU ALREADY HAVE?

First, you have to be aware that you have everything you need in order to be successful, and that the only thing you have to do is change the way you use your tools. As chapter 14 says, *the first steps are always the hardest.* When your mind is conditioned to fail, it's very difficult to convince it to think differently. One of the things I vividly remember when I started my transformation is that, at the beginning, when I was trying to make things work I'd still get the same bad results. Every time that happened I would laugh and tell myself, "I'm now aware of why things didn't work out the way I expected. I take full responsibility, because I know I'm responsible for my results, I'm also aware that my subconscious mind is the one that is making me get these results. This tells me that I still have a lot of work to do to convince my subconscious mind of what I'm capable."

You already have the tools to be successful; how you use them is up to you.

Are you now aware that you have all the tools you need to be successful?

_____

_____

What could you not accomplish, and blamed someone else for your failure?

_____

_____

_____

Based on the situation you're in today, do you think you need to read and learn about personal development or not?

_____

_____

_____

Did your parents use their tools to succeed or to fail, and how did that impact your life?

_____

_____

_____

How do you use your tools when you start a new project? Do you use them for your benefit or against you?

_____

_____

_____

What are you conscious about now that you were not before you read this chapter?

_____

_____

_____

What habits to get better results have you tried to change but failed because you did not see results right away? And what are you going to do differently this time to achieve your goal?

_____

_____

_____

Chapter 18: The Only Way You'll Reach Success Is If You...

☙

DO NOT ALLOW YOUR PAST TO DICTATE YOUR FUTURE.

IT IS A WELL-KNOWN FACT THAT THE FUTURE IS CREATED in the present. Whatever you do today will cause a result that you'll be able to see tomorrow. Some people complain about the results they're getting, but they don't realize that the reason they keep getting the same results over and over is because they keep bringing their past into their present. Since the future is created in the present, and they're bringing their past into their present, tomorrow will look the same as today, yesterday, and all the other days before yesterday.

No matter how long you could have been doing things wrong, the past is history; you can't fix it or change it, but you can always have a better future if you start doing different and better things today.

Remember Joe's story? He'd been working for the same restaurant for years, and kept getting the same pay week after week while he was there. I was talking with Joe one day and he said, "I remember that at my last job I used to open excitedly the envelope that contained my pay check, because I wanted to see how much money I'd made that week. Now, I think about it and feel stupid, because the reason I would open the envelope so eagerly was because I was expecting to see a bigger check; but how could that be possible? How could I expect to make more money when I was working at the same place, doing the same thing, and working the same number of hours?"

Joe's life changed the day he recognized that he was trying to build his future doing the same things he had done in the past. But Joe took action, started doing different things in his present and, as a result of that, he ended up changing not only his future, but his family's future, as well.

NEVER LISTEN TO GOSSIP

Successful people never pay attention to gossip; they don't waste their valuable time in things that don't help them grow.

Gossip is just that, *gossip*. You cannot give your attention to something that doesn't deserve it. One thing is guaranteed, people will always gossip about you, whether you do well or not, whether you try or not. People will always find something to criticize you for. If you want to be successful, focus on your objective and forget about the rest of the world. Successful people do not get distracted by insignificant things.

NEVER SAY *YES*, WHEN YOU REALLY WANT TO SAY *NO*

One of the richest men on Earth, Warren Buffet, says that learning how to say *no* is very important. You don't have to say *yes* to something, when you really want to say *no*.

In order to be able to say *no* to those who want to manipulate you, you have to develop character. You have to be strong enough and learn how not to feel guilty when you say *no* to someone. A lot of people have lost what they had, because of not knowing how to say *no*.

Carlos was the manager of a car dealership where I used to work. One day he came into the lot very happy because he was offered a job at another dealership. He was offered better pay and a two-week vacation in Hawaii for him and his girlfriend. Before he officially moved to his new job, Carlos went on his vacation. When he came back, he started working for the new car lot. Everything was going well for a few months, until one day the owner of the business called Carlos into his office. The owner told Carlos about the problems the company (the dealership) was facing and said that if Carlos accepted to transfer the business to his name—including the debt—he would get compensated, plus a percentage of the sales. Carlos happily accepted, unaware of the owner's real intentions.

About four to five months later, the original owner of the car dealership moved back to his country. The finance manager committed fraud selling the original owner's luxury Lexus to three different finance companies. The finance manager collected the three checks, cashed them, and flew the coop. The dealership was closed by the DMV; Carlos was arrested and ended up behind bars, because he didn't know how to say *no*.

Everything seemed too good to be true and, in fact, it was. By the time Carlos figured out why the owner of the dealership was too nice to him, it was already too late; he was already behind bars.

Don't say *yes* to something, when you really want to say *no*, or else you could end up like Carlos.

At the beginning of my career as a public speaker, I didn't know how to say *no*, and a lot of people involved in network marketing companies took advantage of that. Although I told them I was not interested in joining their company, they'd convince me to go see their presentation, with the promise that they were going to introduce me to their leader and that the company might be interested in my services. It was always the same thing, once the leader realized I was not interested in the business he would find a way to cut me off and leave.

With time, I learned that these people would tell me that just to make me go see their business presentation, hoping that I changed my mind during the meeting.

I knew I had to stop saying *yes* to everything, and had to learn how to say *no* because these people were just playing with my emotions and I was going nowhere. When someone approaches me with the same promise, I tell them, "I want to thank you for thinking of me, but I'm not going to go to your presentation because you're promising something that you know is not possible. You know that, as a multilevel company, you guys have your own trainers and that outside speakers are not allowed." When I tell them that, they usually start saying things like, "You're right, but if you join the company you could have the opportunity to speak in front of thousands of people." So, what they do at the end is to tell me the truth, which convinces me to go to their presentations.

I'm not saying network marketing companies are bad; I know a few people who are doing great doing that kind of business. It's just that multilevel is not my thing.

Learning how to say *no* is one of the most important steps on the road to success.

NEVER ARRIVE LATE

"Eighty percent of success is showing up." ~Woody Allen

Arriving on time gives you credibility. When you're known for arriving on time, it's easier for others to trust you because they know you're reliable.

Successful people never arrive late because they understand the importance of showing up. When you're late, you have to find an excuse, and successful people know excuses are for losers.

When I was working for a training company, I learned a technique to prevent arriving late anywhere. The technique consists of fixing in my mind that the appointment is thirty minutes earlier than it really is. If the appointment is at, let's say, 2:00 PM, I would fix in my mind that the appointment is at 1:30 PM; so I left the office earlier, pretending the appointment was at 1:30 PM, and not at 2:00 PM. This technique helped me be on time 100% of the time. That's right; I was on time for all my appointments.

Some of the benefits I enjoyed from being early included:

1. **I could identify the office where I was going:** This was very helpful, since one of the most common problems when you go to a place where you've never been before is that you might get lost easily, and you don't want that to happen, especially if you don't have plenty of time. When you're pressed for time and, on top of that, you get lost, it is very likely you'll end up being late.

2. **I had plenty of time:** Once I knew where I was going, if I still had some time left, I'd go for a cup of coffee, and used the restroom, if I had to. About fifteen minutes before the actual appointment, I'd get in my car drive to the office where my presentation was going to be, and arrived there on time, relaxed and ready to do my job.

In sales, it is very common to see people looking for good results, but they don't show up to the trainings. Therefore, they don't get the results they're "looking for." I put the words "LOOKING FOR" in quotations marks because there is a big difference between wanting something and taking action to make that *something* happen.

The offices that are getting the best results are the ones that have trainings every week. And the agents who are getting the best results are those who show up to every single meeting. These agents understand the importance of training, and better service for their clients.

A high percentage of people, including a lot of professionals, have a bad habit of arriving late, or not showing up at all.

Remember: Successful people never arrive late because they understand the importance of showing up. When you arrive late you have to find an excuse, and successful people know excuses are for losers.

NEVER INTERRUPT OTHERS

Unsuccessful people like to interrupt others all the time. They usually do it because they think they know everything. I must confess I was one of them for many years, until I realized that if I wanted to learn, I had to keep my mouth shut and my ears open.

That's a habit that is not so easy to overcome because people have so many things inside of them, and they feel they need to bring them out. If you pay attention, you'll notice that these people are always excited, always in a hurry, and have to be right all the time.

The best way to get rid of a bad habit—like interrupting others—is to join groups where discipline is important. In my case, I joined Toastmasters because Toastmasters has rules. One of those rules is to never interrupt the speaker while they're speaking. It was very difficult for me to follow that rule, because I had the habit of interrupting. I did interrupt the speaker on many occasions, but when the General Evaluator would give their report of the meeting, they would always point out my unwanted participation. I was told so many times *not* to interrupt the speaker, that a couple of months later, I was following the rule 100% of the time. It wasn't that I had completely gotten rid of my bad habit, because I still felt the need to opine in the middle of someone else's speech, but I'd stop myself because I knew I had to follow rules. Although it took me some time, I finally got rid of that bad habit.

Successful people do not interrupt because they understand that they learn more by staying quiet.

GET RID OF RESENTMENT

This is probably one of the most important steps on the road to success. No man can go forward carrying his past on his shoulders. Success requires a big jump and you cannot jump when you are carrying something that is too heavy; resentment is not visible, but it weighs tons. I say it because I know; I've lived it.

For twenty-seven years I lived with resentment towards my dad; he mistreated me when I was a kid. My dad is a good man; I only saw him drinking a few times, but he did not have any vices, like smoking, heavy drinking, or anything like that. For years, I had the same question: Why did my dad treat me like that when I was a kid? Why? That question would haunt me. It made me feel bad; it made me remember the bad times, re-live those moments again. That unanswered question made me cry many times.

One day, while I was torturing myself with these thoughts, I had a second of enlightenment and found the answer to the question I'd been asking myself for many years. Right in the midst of my suffering, I thought, "OK. I've always asked myself the same question and I've never understood why my dad treated me the way he did; but let's take a moment to consider his background. My dad didn't have a great life; his mom died when he was only eleven years old, and my grandfather, who was in charge of my father, her sister, and my uncle, treated them very badly."

When I understood my father's life circumstances, something magical happened. I felt different; I felt as if had gotten rid of something. I didn't know what that was, but it was very real. What happened was that I had forgiven my dad; I forgave him when I understood him, when I realized that he had had a very difficult life, too.

Forgiveness is the only method to get rid of resentment.

A lot of people talk about forgiveness, but I think only a few really understand what forgiveness is. One of the definitions of forgiveness that really touched me was given by a speaker who presented at a seminar I attended. He said, "To forgive is not to forget; to forgive is to be able to remember what happened and not feel pain anymore."

To me, that is true because every time I remembered my childhood I'd go back in time and re-live the ugly moments again. This would make me feel bad and I'd cry. To forgive is to be able to remember, but not feel pain anymore.

What are you going to do differently today to start building your future?

_____
_____
_____

When someone speaks ill to you about someone else, do you pay attention to the comments or do you simply ignore them?

_____
_____
_____

Have you ever said *yes* to something when you really wanted to say no? ____. If so, what are you going to do next time you face the same situation?

_____
_____
_____

Do you always arrive on time? _____. If not, what are you going to do to be on time from now on?

_____

_____

_____

Do you have the habit of interrupting? _____. If so, what action are you going to take to discipline yourself in that area?

_____

_____

_____

Do you have resentment towards somebody? If so, why?

_____

_____

_____

What are you going to do to get rid of that resentment? (If it exists.)

_____

_____

_____

Chapter 19: Steps to Reach Your Goal

☙

MAKE A PLAN TO ACCOMPLISH YOUR GOAL.

NOTHING CAN BE ACCOMPLISHED WITHOUT A PLAN. If you want to build a house you need to get the plans (blueprints) approved by the city. You need a plan as a guide to build almost anything, including your goals.

Without a plan, it's almost impossible to accomplish a goal because there is no deadline. When you don't have a date set to accomplish your goal, your mind does not put any pressure on you; there is no commitment.

TAKE ACTION

Most people have plans, but don't take action; and, if they do, it's only for a short period of time. A good example of that is what happens at the beginning of each year. Every year, millions of people buy gym memberships, planning to lose weight. But they go to the gym for only a few weeks. Statistically speaking, 80% of the New Year's Resolutions crowd drops off by the second week of February. This means that only 20% remain, and the rate of sign-ups tapers off by February (almost all of that initial spike, save for, maybe, 1-2% of total volume for the year).

When you decide to take action about something, you cannot stop; you must keep on going or else you are going to fail. Life is like riding a bike: If you stop pedaling you'll inevitably fall. Do you really want to be successful? Remain taking in action; never stop.

You'll be successful the moment you decide that you'll dedicate your entire life to fight for your dreams, and realize that nobody and no circumstances will stop you because you know you are greater than any obstacle that could come your way. Get on the bike of your life today and never stop pedaling; never become too complacent; keep on going until you reach you goal.

BELIEVE IN YOURSELF

When you are on the road to success you'll find a lot of people who will tell you all the reasons why you won't be able to achieve your goal. If you listen to them and you quit, you'll be giving them the pleasure of telling you, "See? I told you so. I knew you couldn't do it." Don't give them that satisfaction. Live for your dream; work for your dream; believe in yourself. There is no power on this Earth that can stop a person who believes in themselves.

It's true that what other people tell you can build you up or destroy you, but what *you* tell yourself will definitely build you up or destroy you. The decision is yours.

PREPARE FOR THE OBSTACLES

When you are prepared for the obstacles, you have a big advantage over most people, because it is here where more than ninety percent will perish. Obstacles are like a test in life; if you fail, guess what? You'll stay in the same classroom for the rest of your life. Obstacles are good because only those who face them are the ones who will see what is on the other side; and what's on the other side of the obstacles is always good.

Have you ever seen a triathlon? Do you know why all the competitors give their best and more during that type of competition? They give their best because all of them are going for the winner's prize. They know what it means and what is at the end of the race. The main reason competitors don't give up before facing the obstacles they have to face is because they know clearly that, in order to be worthy of the prize, they have to overcome all the obstacles.

It's exactly the same in life. The difference is that, in a triathlon, you have an idea of the estimated time it'll take you get to the end of the race, but in life you never know.

All you have to know is that if you're willing to face the obstacles there will be a prize for you at the end; the bigger the obstacles the bigger the prize you'll receive. Don't get discouraged when you see or think that things are getting tough, and always remember: The bigger the obstacles the bigger the reward.

Obstacles discourage people that have a fuzzy idea of what they want. Obstacles give strength to those who have a clear vision of where they're going.

BE CRAZY

Crazy people live in an unrealistic world; crazy people see things other don't; crazy people cannot get along with "normal" people.

When you start thinking outside the box, the people around you start thinking you've lost your mind, and that you must be crazy. They also call you *crazy* because you start talking about things that are not visible or tangible, yet.

When Guglielmo Marconi discovered the aetheric waves (radio waves) and told his family and friends he had found a way to send a message to a distance four miles away, his family and friends thought he was crazy. When the Wright brothers said they were going to make a heavier-than-air object fly, people thought they were crazy, even when they demonstrated that it was possible to make such an object fly. People still saw them as failures because their artifact was in the air for only 12 seconds, and flew a distance of only 120 feet.

In the case of the Wright brothers, people did not take into consideration that they had done something that had never been accomplished before. People focused on what didn't work.

In order to reach success you have to go against the odds; you have to go against the world, against logic. Logically, I should not have been writing this book, but I already know I can go way beyond my limits.

ABOUT THE AUTHOR

ಣ

MOISES OLIVARES IS A MEXICAN IMMIGRANT who came to the United States when he was seventeen. Moises had a lot of dreams and thought coming to the U.S. was the best choice to make lots of money. But when he arrived to Los Angeles and reality hit, he found out that things were not going to be as easy as he thought they would be. Being so young, having no experience in any kind of work, and not speaking a word of English, the only available job he found was selling shaved ice on the streets of the cities of South Gate and Lynwood, California.

Moises disliked that type of job, but that's all he could do because he didn't know any better. Moises was always asking himself, "Is this what I came to the U.S. for, to sell shaved ice on the streets; there has got to be something better out there." With that mindset, Moises started asking his clients if they knew of any job opportunities, and eight months later he finally found someone who helped him to get what he calls his first job; he started working as a frame maker at a furniture company.

Always thinking there had to be something better, Moises also worked as a pizza delivery guy, a truck driver, a car salesman, a Real Estate assistant, and many other jobs. Moises was looking for something, but he didn't know exactly what it was until, one day, he had the opportunity to speak in public. There, Moises found his real passion. He started preparing himself for his passion; he joined Toastmasters to improve his speaking skills, and in 2012 he won 1st

place as the best speaker in the area in a Toastmasters contest. The rest, as they say, is history in the making.

Eventually, Moises was invited to co-write a book called *Descubre TU Grandeza* (Discover Your Greatness) in Spanish. Moises considers that book one of his biggest accomplishments, especially because the book was launched at an event in the Los Angeles Convention Center, with hundreds of people in attendance, and a very special guest: well-known author of the book *The Four Agreements*, Don Miguel Ruiz.

For more information about Moises Olivares and the trainings he offers, log on to MoisesOlvares.com.

GET TRAINED BY MOISES

☙

In order to continue learning from Moises Olivares, and participate in his engaging and informative trainings, in both English and Spanish, please go to MoisesOlvares.com and find out the latest news and information about the upcoming workshops, trainings and seminars.

For a customized training for your team in the topics of Sales, Motivation, Team Building, Leadership and much more, please call toll-free in the United States (888) 854-5467, and ask for Dr. Cesar Vargas, Moises Olivares's Manager.

See you at the top of your journey!

STOP CRYING! GET UP AND TAKE ACTION

ORDER FORM ON THE OTHER SIDE

MOISES OLIVARES

ORDER FORM

I would like to obtain additional copies of ***STOP Crying! Get Up and Take Action*** for me and/or for my family and friends, who are about to change their life through courage and character, and these powerful principles.

Name: _____

Address: _____

City: _____ State: _____

Country: _____ Zip Code: _____

Email (for confirmation purposes): _____

Comments (additional on reverse): _____

Amount _____ X $19.95 (USD)   Subtotal $_____

Shipping & Handling   USA & Canada $ 7.50

                        To Latin America $ 12.50

Email: info@MoisesOlivares.com   Rest of the world   Please Ask

                        Total enclosed (USD) $

Send this form with your remittance to:

VERITAS INVICTUS PUBLISHING
8502 East Chapman Avenue # 302
Orange, California 92869
United States

To obtain your copy via Internet with a credit card, log on to:
www.**Moises***Olivares*.com

www.ingramcontent.com/pod-product-compliance
Lightning Source LLC
Chambersburg PA
CBHW070641050426
42451CB00008B/255